Travels with Buster

A Journey of
Unconditional Love

Diane Viola

'Travels with Buster' is a beautifully conceived memoir of life with a dog. Soul material, charming, so humorous at times I found myself laughing out loud. You are taken on a journey of what it means to fully love, warts and all, in a way that is totally relatable, especially for anyone who has ever loved a dog. Interwoven into the very human and humorous nature of this relatable story are gems of wisdom. As you travel through life with Buster you are painted a sense of the Australian landscape and playground of our K9 friends.

Written in the style of short vignettes, it will touch your heart, and with sweet tenderness remind you of the important things in life. A most delightful read.'

Sharron Brandon

'Travels with Buster' is love on a plate served up with gifts of wisdom, insight and connection that tug at your heart. As proud as any parent can be, Diane leads us on her journey with Buster to laugh, cry and celebrate unconditional love, community and connection for all. An absolutely beautiful read with so many lessons of love, I highly recommend this book for any parent of children and/or fur babies.'

Mary Brock

'As the current owner of a 15+ years furry friend myself, Diane has put into words the absolute joy of caring for a hound from puppy to, for me, close to the end of a much-loved family member's life. Through reading this book I now have a better insight into what lies before me and not only the sadness, but also the positives of my future time with our beloved Jack Russell, Esme. For those of you with a pet reading this book you will relate to and giggle at the antics of Buster as I have. For those of you without, hopefully you will choose to add one to your family to look after and cherish for what is not long enough in a human's life.'

Robert Brown

'I finally finished reading 'Travels with Buster' and although it has taken me longer than I anticipated, I just didn't want to put it down the closer I got to the end. The final version looks fantastic and the photos are great as they add to the personality of Buster that comes through the book.

Even though I never had the opportunity to meet Buster, I feel that through this book there were many lessons to be learnt and there were lots of light-bulb moments. Thank you, Diane. I've read lots of self-help books but this would be among the best of them. You should be so proud of your achievement.'

Vivien Krepp

'A heart-warming tale reminding us of what is truly important in life. Buster is indeed an amazing teacher!'

Beth Phelan
Conference Director, Happiness & Its Causes

'A lovely balance of sharing, empathy and gentle teaching. Your natural gift as a true teacher is most poignantly reflected here in your absolute willingness to be the student, to be vulnerable and to receive the lessons that life and Buster offer you.'

Pete Sheldon

'I loved your book! You have a beautiful way of telling a story and I found myself watching Buster in my mind's eye. Thank you for allowing me to share in your memories of Buster and what you learnt by having him in your life. I am so pleased to have known him and will always remember Mr. Buster with great love and affection.

You have done a wonderful job that many people will not only enjoy, but will use in their growth as a parent, a friend and companion.'

Julie Webb

Travels with Buster: A Journey of Unconditional Love

Copyright © Diane Viola 2018

www.dianeviola.com

The moral rights of Diane Viola to be identified as the author of this work have been asserted in accordance with the Copyright Act 1968.

First published in Australia 2018 by Positive Relating

www.positiverelating.com

ISBN 978-0-6484054-0-5

All rights reserved. No part of this publication may be reproduced, stored in a retrieval system, or transmitted in any form or by any means, electronic, photocopy, recording or otherwise, without prior written permission of the author. Nor can it be circulated in any form of binding or cover other than that in which it is published and without similar condition including this condition being imposed on a subsequent purchaser.

Disclaimer

All the information, techniques, skills and concepts contained within this publication are of the nature of general comment only, and are not in any way recommended as individual advice. The intent is to offer a variety of information to provide a wider range of choices now and in the future, recognising that we all have widely diverse circumstances and viewpoints. Should any reader choose to make use of the information herein, this is their decision, and the author and publisher/s do not assume any responsibilities whatsoever under any conditions or circumstances. The author does not take responsibility for the business, financial, personal or other success, results or fulfilment upon the readers' decision to use this information. It is recommended that the reader obtain their own independent advice.

Dedicated to my mother who understood the depth of love Roberto and I shared with Buster, was always attentive to my funny stories about him and ready to welcome him into Heaven with potato chips.

'Until one has loved an animal a part of one's soul remains unawakened.'

Anatole France

Contents

Introduction 1

Stage One – Puppy Power 10

1. The Journey Begins 13
2. Two-Pointed Intention 16
3. We Are Family 19
4. Love's Invisible Thread 25
5. Relinquishing Control 29
6. Water Baby Buster 33
7. Through the Eyes of a Child 39

Stage Two – Childhood & Adolescence 44

8. Making Friends, Losing Friends 47
9. The Gentle Art of Persuasion 53
10. Personal Power 57
11. Buster the Swimming Champ 61
12. Buster's Run, Forging Pathways of Change ... 68
13. I Won't Let You Forget (Me) 72
14. All is Right in the World Again 78

Stage Three – Adulthood & Independence 82

15. Lessons in Compassion 85

16. Time-Out for Fun! 89

17. Up for the Challenge 94

18. My Ears Hurt When You Speak That Way 100

19. Mind Your Manners 104

20. Developing Self-Discipline 109

21. Attention Absolute 114

Stage Four – The Final Chapter 118

22. Everyone Loves Buster 121

23. Mummy's Little Helper 126

24. The Things We Do for Love 136

25. Warning Signs 140

26. The Importance of Trusting Yourself 146

27. Time to Say Goodbye 153

28. The Gift of Life 166

Conclusion 174

Reflections from Buster 176

Acknowledgements 178

About the Author 182

Introduction

> *'There can be no keener revelation of a society's soul than the way in which it treats its children.'*
>
> **Nelson Mandela**

This book is a collection of stories about Buster, my life with him and how that relates to all of our lives. Looking back, I am so grateful that he was sent to me to help me through the challenges I was presented with as I entered a whole new stage of my life. I'm not sure who led whom and I do know we were meant to do this together.

As you will read, for my husband, Roberto, and me, Buster was our four-legged boy and in many ways, this is also our story. Despite living beyond his 15th year, exceeding the expected life-span for his breed by 18 months, Buster's passing on 27 December, 2017 has represented the loss of our only 'child' and the feelings which accompany that.

Whilst I did pre-warn people in the early days of my penchant for telling stories about Buster, eventually a time came when the focus of my conversation was not all about him and the latest antics he'd gotten up to. My concern that I may have become somewhat obsessed was allayed by the recognition that this banter was my way of sharing the joy I was experiencing in my new-found role as mother to a staffy x kelpie who had the best of both breeds. A fun junkie is how I described him; at other times, my fitness coach.

Having previously written peer-led personal development and anti-bullying programs for children and young people, and copious articles on relationship, parenting and family life, my intention was to write a book that would appeal to seekers of all ages, from young adults to centenarians. I would be delighted to think that I have been successful in fulfilling that purpose. Throughout my working life, my commitment has always been to the welfare of those among us who are our most vulnerable and most valuable: our children. I see them as 'Children of the World' and the responsibility for raising them to be a shared one, for our future does, indeed, depend on them.

A phenomenon of recent decades are the children who have been managing upwards, with parents who have sought to be their friends, often resulting in out of control and angry young people who are,

Introduction

indeed, too big for their boots and in need of guidance from their elders. We need to get back in our place and fulfil our role as our children's first teachers so that they can receive the parenting and unconditional love they need to be able to take their place in the world as healthy adults. At the same time, for many of us, our first job must be to re-parent ourselves; to give ourselves the unconditional love and positive regard that was missing in our own childhood experience. Only then can we truly give with the open heart that is required of us on this most challenging and rewarding of journeys.

Despite completing the Conceptual Framework for this book in January 2005, when Buster had been with us for less than two years, and my mother's repeated encouragement to just get on and write it, as it turned out, I would have to travel through the whole of Buster's life with him before I could finally complete it. I had always envisaged Buster sitting beside me on the floor as I signed copies of the book at the Book Launch and at subsequent events if I was fortunate enough for it to be a success. While I know it won't be the same, I do trust that he will be there, as he is now, with me in Spirit. Apart from the actual demands of life itself, once confronted with the loss of both my mother and my 'son', Buster, less than six months apart in 2017, and with my 60th birthday looming large, writing this book became my top priority. It has also been at times both the most joyous and most painful thing I have ever done with a 'million' tears or more cried in the process.

Among my many attempts to make a start on this book was the day that became the subject of the story that follows here:

> 'Oh, the simplicity of life! Finally sitting beneath the tree on our property that gives me a clear view from my husband's workshop down to the creek; comfortably set up in a folding armchair, bottle of water at my side and the ever-faithful Buster at my feet, ready to begin to write this book in earnest after seemingly so many interruptions. After a delayed start, my notebook, the one I have so loved for its ability to offer me the freedom to write in this way, switches into gear. As I open the files to 'Travels with Buster' I think -
>
> Returning to my spot beneath the tree after re-charging my battery, with yet more thoughts in mind of how to begin, what should occur but for the 'star' of this book to act completely out of character and **leave** the safety of our property to pursue a boy on his bike from the grass verge outside. "Yet more fodder for the book," I think. A mother's work is never done and I didn't imagine for a

moment that the nature of the beast wouldn't override all my teaching if something more enticing should present itself. I'm pleased to say that the chastisement he received was sufficient to keep him at rest on the other side of the tree when, only a matter of minutes later, a motorbike came zooming by. All of this had made a liar of me as, in response to the question not more than an hour or so before from a neighbour – "Does he ever run away any more?" – I had proudly answered in the negative.'

The thought that Buster's antics had intruded upon was this: "Isn't the victory in pursuing your passion all the sweeter when it follows on the tails of having to repeatedly clear the blocks to one's path?". I wonder if that's the way we human beings find out just how serious we really are about what we want, or want to do? If there was hesitation, doubt, lack of trust or faith in the chosen path, all the obstacles over which we must step to get there enable us to crystallise our intent and commitment to it. The sublime irony in this is that I had to leave my home and go away on a holiday that turned out to be anything but that, in order to come back home again and discover that everything I needed was already there, just waiting for me to embrace it. I had laughingly told people that Buster and I were going off to a

Caravan Park for four days so that, out of actually travelling with Buster, I could start writing my book. Now, that was an adventure in itself!

'Travels with Buster: A Journey of Unconditional Love' is arranged into four sections, loosely corresponding to the four stages of Buster's life in the homes we lived in during that time. Whilst I would encourage you to read it in order, you could also read any chapter that appeals to you independent of the others, although it may not be as much fun! Of necessity, some of the stories span more than one period and place in time. While it is inspired by the events I recount of his life, this is clearly not 'just' a book about a dog! I invite you to take the time to reflect on what each chapter means for you and your life and the emotions it evokes in you.

In the pages of this book, I trust you will find sprinkles of the humour and light-heartedness that inspired its writing. I recall soon after conceiving of it, long before I was able to truly devote myself to its writing, seeing a story about Shirley MacLaine's then-new book 'Out on a Leash'. I thought at the time that, as an acclaimed actress and author, she would no doubt attract many readers to it, however her dog appeared to be no match for my Buster! I admit that, like most other books written about dogs others have mentioned to me, I have not read it, however, I see she too has now suffered the loss of her dog, Terry, which she shares in the revised edition of her book. I took the stand to honour the story within me about my beloved Buster, the meaning that I was to bring to these pages and the messages I wanted to share with my readers. If there is one thing I know and respect, it is that everyone who loves their dog (or other furry or feathered animal) as I do, will have a mountain of funny, heart-warming stories to tell, perhaps even similar to the experiences I share about my boy. I would encourage them to do as I have done if the calling within them is strong enough. But be warned … it may be a journey from which you will not return the same!

My intention with this book is that it will nurture you, touch your heart and reignite your passion for life, love and all who are dear to you, in whatever form they take. None of us is going to get out of this thing alive! So, while we're here, we need to make the most of it, to experience life with all its gifts; of joy and sadness, of giving and receiving, of light and darkness, of the courage that comes from 'seeing things as they are and being willing to meet life on its own terms' and of the strength that comes from the practice of gentleness. These are the gifts bestowed on me as I traversed this journey of unconditional love with Buster that gave me the trust and faith to engage in the swings and roundabouts of life! May you too be blessed with a little of this magic as you travel the pages of this book in your own imagination.

Pure and simple – that's a dog's life! And that is the gift Buster was and continues to be, to me, which I now offer to you, with love.

Diane Viola & Buster in Spirit

When we were very young ...

Stage One
Puppy Power

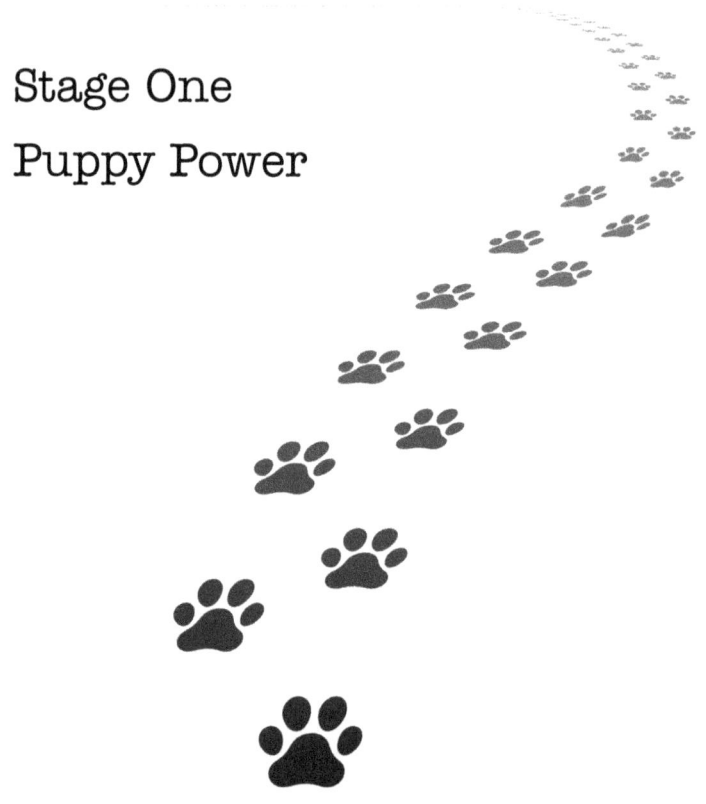

Banora Point | Tweed Valley | NSW
April 2003–March 2004

Chapter 1.
The Journey Begins

'And think not you can direct the course of love, for love, if it finds you worthy, directs your course.'

Khalil Gibran

"Stop! He's come to teach us about unconditional love." These words were my plea to my husband, Roberto, to cease his discipline when Buster, our then 4-month-old staffy x kelpie puppy, had destroyed two pairs of my shoes. It was one of the first times we had left him alone since bringing him home from the RSPCA as an abandoned puppy. Ignorant of the strength and determination of a creature who weighed in at no more than 10 kilograms, it was beyond all reason that, while we were out, he'd be able to push aside our rather hefty BBQ and jump up onto the railing of the balcony to bring down two pairs of near-new shoes drying in the sun, supposedly away from his playful reach. We were soon to discover that, like babies cutting their teeth, there was no end to the gnawing need he had to chew, chew, chew. Rocks, irrigation pipes and rotting staircase all fell victim to the strength of his teeth.

Far from wanting to hurt Buster, as he slapped a rolled-up newspaper into his own hand, Roberto's intention was instead to teach him that what he had done was unacceptable. Nonetheless, Buster was still a 'baby' and this was our opportunity to be bigger than our initial, automatic reactions.

That morning, I experienced for the first time the power of motherhood. Why had Buster destroyed my shoes and left Roberto's intact? This was my introduction to the idea that I was No.1 in his life; his carer, his mum, his protector and even though that was to change over time, as it is meant to, it was my job to step up into that role. So, when he ruined my favourite sandals and jelly clogs, to my surprise, it was not punishment or retribution I sought, but rather understanding. This was natural to him; he was a puppy after all and I was his mum, the one with whom he had bonded.

Despite the disfigurement of my shoes, which at the time I could ill-afford to replace, this was his way of staying close to me; of asserting his right

Chapter 1. The Journey Begins

to his place in my life. Here was the opportunity to do what all parents are called upon to do – to give love unconditionally – which, at the end of the day, is the only love there is. Buster had already begun to be our greatest teacher and with that a calm surrounded us all and a new chapter opened in our lives. Roberto and I had become parents and Buster had made us a family. There would be much to learn.

Chapter 2.
Two-Pointed Intention

> *'You do not need to leave your room. Remain sitting at your table and listen. Do not even listen, simply wait, be quiet, still and solitary. The world will freely offer itself to you to be unmasked, it has no choice, it will roll in ecstasy at your feet.'*
>
> **Franz Kafka**

I first learnt about 'One-Pointed Intention' from Deepak Chopra. I understood it to be a powerful way of attracting into your life the things you desire with least effort and an attitude of detachment to the outcome. It wasn't until Buster came on the scene, however, that I witnessed this concept to its greatest effect. The advantage Buster had over we humans was that his was a 'Two-Pointed Intention'!

Chapter 2. Two-Pointed Intention

Dogs are creatures of habit and routine. Like children, they function best within its parameters of certainty. Buster's bedtime routine involved a last play for the day outside, going to the toilet and saying goodnight, before bouncing into his kennel, frozen chook neck or wing between his teeth. Whilst bedtime was generally around 9.00-9.30 pm, his body clock was invariably more reliable than either mine or Roberto's attention to the clock on the wall. When the time had come, Buster would enter the doorway of the room we were sitting in and, with a body that never quite grew to match the size of his two pointy ears, he would sit motionless and at times expressionless, directing his attention and energy toward us. With ears pointed heavenwards, he would sit patiently waiting until we noticed his presence and responded to his silent request.

His ability to inspire action on our part was enhanced by the gentleness and persistence with which he appealed to our sense of duty. It never ceased to astound me how he could get his message across without so much as opening his mouth to make a sound. Among the more joyful evenings were the ones when, desirous of play, he would bring first one, then another and then finally a third of his beloved toys and sit with them either in his mouth or at his feet as if to say, "Okay, so will this one do?" Focused on his intent, never doubting that the outcome was assured, he epitomised the words in Franz Kafka's quote above.

What he also demonstrated was his absolute expectation and preparedness to receive that which he desired. Of course, it helped that he had come to trust that his needs and wants, simple as they were, would be fulfilled even when he was in the care of someone other than Roberto or myself. That trust – that his or her parents will meet a child's needs – is fundamental to the healthy development of the child. A child who is dependent on its parents for its basic needs, learns to value and meet their own needs once they are old enough because they have experienced the dependability with which their parents have applied themselves to this task. Had Buster experienced neglect or ongoing disruption to his routine, he may have been less certain of his place or the outcome of his requests. Knowing he was loved, he never had to question that his needs would be attended to and for us the giving was always a joyous act.

Chapter 3.
We Are Family

'Children learn about the nature of the world from their family. They learn about power and about justice, about peace and about compassion within the family. Whether we oppress or liberate our children in our relationships with them will determine whether they grow up to oppress and be oppressed or to liberate and be liberated.'

Desmond Tutu

Whenever Roberto and I tell the story of the day we brought Buster home, we're reminded of just how daft we humans can sometimes be! While we hadn't anticipated actually bringing a little puppy home that day, we were united in our thoughts that the small shed at the furthest reaches of our backyard would make an ideal place for Buster to sleep at night. Ill-prepared as we were, we surmised that he would be out of the elements, warm and safe from harm. So, when the time came, we set him up with everything we thought he would need for the night, closed the door behind him and went back into the house. Even as I write this I'm chuckling to myself and imagining you've already guessed what happened next. Yes … it was no surprise that within no time at all, out of the mouth of this little babe came wailing cries! Innocent as was our intent, it was a fairly naive thing to do! Given we had just acquired him from the RSPCA, the last of his litter to be claimed after being abandoned in a cardboard box by the side of the road, the last thing he would have wanted was to have been left alone yet again.

Very quickly, a decision to not bring him into the house retreated to one of compassion and the recognition that he was, indeed, now a member of our family and deserved to have a place in our home. As we were unaware of just how well house-trained he already was and not yet ready for him to sleep inside the house itself, we chose a compromise that enabled him to sleep soundly that first night on the balcony just outside the kitchen, still close enough to feel our presence. And so began the steady decline: from sleeping outdoors, to the garage and finally to sleeping – and snoring – in the bedroom with us. With

Chapter 3. We Are Family

each move to a new home, what had previously been suitable bedding was no more and things were adjusted to meet the requirements of his wellbeing and safety. Cane toads, snakes and acreage made for not only a slightly more dangerous backyard, but also one whose night air temperature would play havoc with his hip dysplasia.

The one boundary we were unanimous in our agreement on was that he would never sleep on our bed. Now, as you know, for every rule, there is an exception and Buster was not about to break with convention! While he never asked to come up onto our bed or attempted to cross that boundary, there was a brief moment in time when he came very close. At the time, we were living in the Bonogin Valley and Julie, my oldest friend, was visiting from Sydney. From their first meeting, Julie referred to him as 'Mr Buster' and theirs was a mutually affectionate, loving relationship. We were all at home one Sunday afternoon just relaxing while Buster was hanging out with Julie in her room. As I walked past the guest bedroom I caught a glimpse of Buster out of the corner of my eye through the open doorway. To my surprise, there he was sitting up on the bed beside Julie with an expression on his face that to this day gladdens my heart. When we made eye contact, his face had the most priceless, quizzical expression on it; definitely one of those moments when a picture told a thousand words or more. It was a combination of disbelief and denial – like he was shrugging his shoulders saying – "I was only being polite, she asked me up after all!" or "It's not how it looks, I'm just visiting." Unsure if I'd actually seen what I thought I had, I did a double-take to confirm it before heading in to the garage to consult with Roberto. When I told Roberto and asked whether we should let him stay there or not, his response was a resounding "No!"

It was one of those times where no one was in the wrong; it was just a difference of experience and expectation. Prior to this, Julie hadn't been told of our preference and Buster had never been given the opportunity to challenge it. For us, as it is for any parent, this was the testing ground to see how we would respond. Once the line had been crossed, albeit innocently, we had the choice to laugh it off and let him remain on the bed, thereby negating what we had already determined as a boundary we wanted to keep, or to follow through by asking Buster to get off the bed.

When I returned to the room and let Julie and Buster know what the house rules were, he was removed from the bed at once. While I imagine he was quite comfortable staying just where he was, I think he too was wondering whether he

Chapter 3. We Are Family

should have been there or not and his demeanour suggested that he was pleading innocence, leaving Julie to pay the price for such an indiscretion. Nonetheless, this event cemented their relationship and became one of those funny stories we loved to tell, a precious shared memory for us all.

Buster's expression that day reminded me of those times when a toddler does something they know they shouldn't have and feign ignorance. You know, like the butter-wouldn't-melt-in-their-mouth child hiding a broken or 'stolen' toy behind their backs who, when asked what they're holding, smile sweetly, eyes giving away the truth, and reply "Nothing!" Or the one who walks out of your bathroom, face and mirror covered in lipstick and gives the same answer when asked what they've been up to. No doubt you have your own stories to tell! As adults and parents, we're usually torn between the urge to burst out laughing and the desire to keep our composure just long enough to express our disapproval at the offence or the lies that accompany them. Most often we need to walk away and let it all out first before being up for the job of a straight-faced disciplinarian.

In any case, apart from a period where we did invite him up for cuddles on the lounge (once it was adequately covered), this was the one and only time Buster ever found his way onto a bed inside the house. As for the surprises that were to come once we had an outdoor living area? Well, that's a story for another day!

Chapter 4.
Love's Invisible Thread

'When you walk across the fields with your mind pure and holy, then from all the stones, and all growing things, and all animals, the sparks of their soul come out and cling to you, and then they are purified and become a holy fire in you.'

Ancient Hasidic Saying

The day I returned home to find the side gate ajar and the yard empty was my first real confrontation with the possibility of loss, of losing my beloved Buster. He was just a tiny little puppy and our bond was still in the formative stages. He had a lovely backyard to play in and we lived in a cul-de-sac off a cul-de-sac; a quiet, peaceful street mid-way up the hill with a beautiful outlook to the Pacific Ocean and, most importantly, one that was safe from passing traffic. With just six houses in our little street, it was an ideal place to raise a child, two-legged or four.

Just love those tiny legs and floppy, puppy ears!

Although I couldn't put my finger on it at the time, while I was out, I knew that something was wrong. I could feel that all was not well. In this first instance, the feeling wasn't strong enough to alter my behaviour, however I know that I was anxious to get home and ensure that everything was okay.

So, when I arrived home to find Buster missing, it was hard to hold back the tears as I started running around our street, calling out his name. Despite using my teacher's voice, at first there was no reply from Buster. Luckily, as it was such a small area to search, he soon responded to my calls and I followed the sound of his bark to the house three

Chapter 4. Love's Invisible Thread

doors away. I can still see his little face peeping out from between the hedges, as he crouched there, not knowing what to do, his eyes wide open as he stared back at me. The relief I felt was beyond my comprehension; what would I have done if something had happened to him or he'd been lost for good? Crying with relief I picked him up and carried him home, both of us a little shattered from the experience.

On that day, as far as I can tell, the side fence had blown open and, wanting to satisfy his curiosity, Buster had ventured out beyond the yard and didn't know exactly how to get back again. Interestingly, a couple of years later as a full-grown dog in our next home, he would sneak out and run around the corner to his friend's house to play, often returning unaccompanied before I had even discovered he was missing. There was many a phone call between myself and his friend Didi's mum, Christine, letting the other know that our 'boys' were safely playing together in each other's yards. On this occasion, however, it became very clear just how easily things can go awry, as well as how to begin to trust the feeling that let would let me know. I came to think of this connection with Buster as 'love's invisible thread'; the thing that connected us wherever we were. I am sure all parents feel this with their children, whether they are consciously aware of it or not.

From that day onward, whenever I was away from Buster and had that niggling feeling, I would inwardly tell him that I loved him and would be home soon, or, if that wasn't the case, that he would be looked after by whomever he was in the care of at the time. We are all, always connected, whether we know it, or believe it, or feel it, or not. Love's invisible thread unites us and brings us peace, especially with those who have travelled across the Rainbow Bridge to another time and place. It is this that tells us we are never really alone, that everything we need is always there waiting in the wings for us and encourages us to have faith, to keep going and to reach out to others when they are in need, as well as to ask for help when we need it ourselves.

Chapter 5. Relinquishing Control

'Radical acceptance rests on letting go of the illusion of control and a willingness to notice and accept things as they are right now, without judging.'

Marsha M. Linehan

One of the most valuable and life-changing lessons I learnt long before Buster came into my life, was that, despite my good intentions, I had absolutely no control over anything or anyone outside myself. A sobering discovery. I was first introduced to this concept in 1985 while teaching children with a range of physical, intellectual and emotional disabilities in country New South Wales; a position which certainly kept me on my toes and one I am glad I was young and fit enough to handle at the time. Each of the children I taught was an extraordinary teacher themselves in what they brought forth in others and Trevor (a pseudonym) was no exception. Just six years old when I first began working with him, he had managed to gain a reputation for being fairly difficult to handle. After Trevor upturned one doctor's office, he proclaimed that anyone who could teach him deserved a Victoria Cross. Whilst I was never awarded such a tribute, I did indeed teach him. My ability to do so came from being able to see who he really was beyond the behaviours he displayed to throw unsuspecting folk off guard.

When I went to the States early in 1985 to do one of the Personal Growth courses popular at the time, I had already spent more than a year struggling to get Trevor to comply. Somewhere in the proceedings of that week-long course, I realised that the more I attempted to get him to toe the line, the more he resisted me and the further away I was from understanding what was really driving his behaviour. The realisation that it was not my job, nor was it possible to control another person, was both the most liberating and instructive gift I received. It became the distinction that allowed me to be my most effective and humane in both my personal and professional life thereafter.

On returning to Australia, I was immediately able to incorporate this into how I worked with

Chapter 5. Relinquishing Control

my students and the results were impressive. What I had previously sought to change actually became the means by which I could connect with children who were mostly non-verbal and relied on other behaviours to communicate their needs and wants. Now the dastardly flicker of the eyes alerted me to a desire to engage or play, rather than as something to fear. We began to recognise Trevor's latent abilities where previously we had seen only misbehaviour. This was yet another reminder that all of our behaviour is purposeful. With this renewed understanding of our basic nature, and the mutual respect that ensued between myself and my students, it became easier to put boundaries and guidelines in place for a more harmonious classroom environment in both regular and special schools.

With this awareness under my belt, when Buster came along I was able to benefit from many years of practice in not needing to control the behaviour of others. Whilst he was something of a star at Puppy Pre-School and Middle School, observing him on our morning walks simply doing what a dog does, I saw no need to try to make him do what I wanted him to. Something of a rebel myself, there was nothing appealing to me about being regimental with him. At the same time, I actually had very little if any difficulty controlling him because I could use my teacher's voice and my own practice of one-pointed intention to let him know I meant business if it was necessary. Interestingly, I only made the connection between the words 'follow your nose' when we commenced our walks together. Until I observed Buster sniffing back and forth and every which way to follow his nose, I had been unaware that there was indeed a literal meaning to the saying. While fellow dog-lovers would jokingly ask who was leading who, I was happy to accept that these walks were for Buster and his enjoyment. I could take myself wherever I wanted whenever I chose, but he was dependent on myself or Roberto to take him out for walks and he deserved to be free to wander where he chose within the limits of what was safe and comfortable for us all.

The need for power and control is an all-pervasive one for human-beings. When we are in touch with our personal power and have control over our own actions, there is no need to have power over or to attempt to control, others. There is a vast difference between obedience or compliance that comes from fear and the spirit of cooperation that is the result of mutual understanding and respect. In letting go of the need to control, we were able to be more relaxed as parents and this allowed us to take delight in observing Buster being true to his nature as a dog and all the surprises that came with that.

Chapter 6.
Water Baby Buster

'I am blessed to have been born in Australia where water sports are loved and swimmers are revered.'

Shane Gould

If there was one thing Buster loved, it was swimming. And over the course of his lifetime, he was blessed to have a plethora of wonderful places to immerse himself in that pleasure. The water was a passion we shared as a family, although our preferences were varied.

Roberto always felt more comfortable on top of the water and, prior to meeting me, led an enviable life as a Master Class 5 Skipper chartering yachts through the Mediterranean and Caribbean. I still ask myself "What were you thinking?" when I declined Roberto's offer to sell up here and take up the yachting life ourselves, which had been his original intention when he returned to Australia in late 1986 after his first visit the Christmas before. If things had gone according to his plan, he would have opened an Italian Restaurant here, made a bucket of money and bought his own yacht to begin a charter business in the Caribbean Islands with the spoils of the sale. Instead, he married me and made his life in Australia. Interestingly, in doing so, he fulfilled the destiny that had been meant for his mother and her family. Some decades earlier, their own voyage to this country had been foiled by an opportunist, who stole all their belongings from Roberto's newly-widowed grandmother on the dock just as they were preparing to leave Italy. Needless to say, Roberto's Nonna became,

Chapter 6. Water Baby Buster

if she was not already, a strong, resilient woman who opened her own retail business and made a new life for herself and her children in Milano. While in the early days of our relationship I carried a feeling of guilt for having kept Roberto from fulfilling his Caribbean dream, when I found myself pushing him away so that he could be free to pursue it, he assured me that our being married and the family we would build together was the future he had already chosen.

It took some years for me to be able to accept that Roberto's choice would not be something he would later regret, or hold against me. I'm now certain that the answer I gave 30 years ago is being manifest in the life I am living and the writing of this book, with Buster's life being the greatest gift to us both. When sailing the high seas was no longer an option for Roberto, he went back to school and learnt how to surf at the 'tender' age of 35. Un-phased by being the eldest in his class of 7-9-year old's, on Sydney's Collaroy Beach, he demonstrated the great spirit of having a go that was later to be mirrored in our boy's behaviour.

Swimming was the sport I felt most accomplished in from my school days. It was also the one exercise I recall sharing with my own family as a child, when we would all go to the local swimming pool for early morning training. As children, we were members of a swimming squad and Saturday mornings were spent in competition races followed by devouring what I recall were the longest, hottest and tastiest sausage rolls, smothered in tomato sauce. My father was a strong swimmer although his stroke was less refined than my mother's. He spoke often of the river he swam and dived into as a child in his village in Northern Lebanon. Dad took great pride in running beside us, egging us on as we swam in our club and school competition events, and would go wild with excitement whenever any of us won a place, my sister, Loretta, the most likely candidate for a first.

For the 15 years before Buster came to us, Roberto and I lived within cooee of some of Australia's most beautiful beaches, in the Northern Beaches of Sydney and later the Tweed and Gold Coasts. Walking, swimming and surfing in the ocean were an integral part of our lives. Both Cancerians, our love of water and affinity with it came naturally and Buster seemed to embrace that too, like so many other dogs we met along the way. Given that we adopted Buster when he was around 4 months old, we missed seeing his first stumbling steps into life. The closest parallel to this was the occasion of Buster's first swim. Despite having had a number

Chapter 6. Water Baby Buster

of dogs as pets, albeit for brief periods of time, I had never seen them swim and was unaware of just how naturally that skill came to dogs.

So, when I took Buster to the nearest enclosure with still water on a warm, late August winter's day, I approached this with the same caution as I had some years before when teaching students with a disability to swim. For the first few steps I allowed him to walk into the water unaided and he was clearly happy to be there. As soon as the shoreline dropped away, I picked him up and carried him to where the water was waist height, making it comfortable for me to stand with him in my arms. I remember putting my hand under his tummy to hold him up and without a second's hesitation, his little legs sprang into action as if they'd just been waiting for the moment when they could walk this way. Trusting that he would stay afloat, as I let him go to have his first swim, I let out a scream of delight. To see him just take-off like that, swimming for the first time so naturally, effortlessly and joyfully, was one of the most delightful moments of my life and served as the catalyst for ensuring that he would enjoy this activity throughout his own.

We were fortunate that swimming came easily to Buster and it was only later that I discovered that not all dogs can swim or take to the water with the same excitement as our 'water baby' did. For

Buster in Bliss!

much of his life he was able to swim if not daily, at least on a weekly basis, which really helped to keep him fit and strong and curtail the effects of his hip dysplasia. No doubt the distances he was able to swim, whether just for his own pleasure or in pursuit of a stick, also helped to keep his heart and lungs in optimal condition. In creeks, rivers, lakes, beaches, waterholes and swimming pools, Buster found a way to keep cool, have fun and stay mobile.

Chapter 7. Through the Eyes of a Child

'Sometimes', said Pooh, 'the smallest things take up the most room in your heart.'

A. A. Milne

Over the years, and of necessity when he began sleeping in our bedroom, Buster acquired a large collection of beds for both day and night. However, there were two we purchased at the very beginning that saw him through the whole of his life, which we still have today. One is in the cargo area of my SUV and the other just outside the back door, in case his Spirit comes to visit. Just like the ears he never fully grew into, we overestimated how big he would be once he had finished growing, and so his day-bed and kennel were always one size too big for his medium-sized body. Nonetheless, while the former provided safe carriage for him in my car of the day, there was no place he loved to be, or felt more like home for Buster, than his kennel. It was where he took his treats and bones to chew, made an almighty ruckus bouncing toys off the roof and walls, rummaged around and got lost in the folds of his blankie and rested his little chin on the edge as he stared out at the world. And, of course, where he enjoyed the hedonistic pleasure of a squillion peaceful hours of sleep!

Despite how much we loved living in our first home up here, our purpose in leaving Sydney in 2002 had been to find a little property where we could each work from home and have the freedom to fulfil our creative pursuits; Roberto making fine furniture and me working with clients and writing. So, even though we had lived in Banora Point for only a brief time, when the landlord for Roberto's workshop announced that he wasn't going to renew the lease, the motivation to find our dream-home, complete with workshop and studio, became more urgent. For Buster this meant that by the time we were ready to move, he had lived there for just shy of a year.

In our first home, Buster's kennel was not just his daytime castle but also where he slept at night, so it made sense that he would have been rather

Chapter 7. Through the Eyes of a Child

attached to it. On the day we moved house, it should have come as no surprise to us that he may have a little separation-anxiety. He was still such a tiny puppy, especially in contrast to the burly Removalists who came to empty our house that day. No doubt, he would already have been confused and disoriented by all the activity and noise. But when one of the Removalists picked up his kennel and started walking away with it, he let out the most heart-wrenching cry. While our main concern was to keep him safe and ensure that he didn't get under anyone's feet or hurt himself, we had not foreseen the impact our move would have on this little bunny. It was as if once more he was being uprooted and all he could say was, "Don't take my home away from me!"

This home had become his stability, his kennel the centre of his world and out of nowhere it looked as if it was all being taken away. With lots of cuddles and words of comfort he made it through and we learned valuable lessons for the moves which were to follow. So often in our busy lives we either take for granted or fail to notice that it's the smallest things that mean the most to us and that the smaller we are, the bigger those little things appear!

Like all children, Buster craved – and thrived on – routine, stability and the known. Dependent on the adults in their lives and by association, at the mercy of the choices they make, what allows a child to feel a measure of control are solid foundations and a sense that they can trust and count on the people in their lives. These are essential to healthy growth and development and the building blocks of resilience. This certainty and the confidence that accompanies it, enhances their ability to face life's problems, disappointments and challenges, as well as to embrace new opportunities when they present themselves.

By the time we left the Tweed Valley, we had discovered more than a dozen beautiful walks we could choose from and, in preparation for leaving, I ensured we re-visited each of them to say our goodbyes. Interestingly, one of our favourites, the walk along Dreamtime Beach at the far northern end of Kingscliff, was also where we had our second-to-last family holiday many years later. True to his habit of bringing sticks home from our walks, it was in the park just across the road from our holiday accommodation that Buster found the stick which would become his 'trusted friend' and on which he rested his chin for the last two years in his beloved kennel. Unlike all the other sticks he'd claimed, this was never used for catch and to this day has its home inside his kennel.

Chapter 7. Through the Eyes of a Child

Soon after Buster passed, needing time-out and nurturing, Roberto and I spent a few days in that same motel, giving us, myself in particular, time to release more of the sadness and give thanks to the places that had blessed us with so many joyous memories.

I'm a big boy now! ...

Stage Two

Childhood & Adolescence

Bonogin | Gold Coast Hinterland | QLD

March 2004-October 2009

Chapter 8. Making Friends, Losing Friends

> *'Don't walk behind me; I may not lead. Don't walk in front of me; I may not follow. Just walk beside me and be my friend.'*
>
> **Albert Camus**

If there's one thing that sustains us in life, it is our friends and family. While dogs are said to be 'Man's Best Friend', for most of us who have a dog, they are also our family and we their pack. What constitutes friendship, how we sustain and nurture them and what we do when friendships change or we lose a friend or family member, are fundamental aspects of what makes for a harmonious life.

Rocco was a rather lonely looking dog who spent most of his day tied to a somewhat short rope outside the window of the kitchen facing toward the street. Buster, who always managed to have compassion for the underdog, made a point of stopping by to say hello and spend a little time with Rocco on our morning walks in Banora Point. In fact, if he hadn't seen him for a while, he'd be certain to drag me there at lightning speed all the way from home. The day they finally got to play unhampered by ropes or leads, Buster ran circles around Rocco with excitement and joy. On this day the commotion drew Rocco's mum outside and it was in conversation with her that I learned the reason that Rocco was so restricted. Unfortunately, Rocco's backyard was unsuitable for him to play in and the family was subsequently moving to a more appropriate home.

The first time we visited after Rocco had moved, Buster's response was one of utter disbelief. "I've come to visit and you're not home! How can that be?" Obviously, his spot beside the house still carried his scent and, for some time after that, each time we passed the house I had to console Bustie that his friend Rocco was there no more.

I imagine some months later Buster had become a little better adapted to people or his friends moving on in life. The brown pony, whom he befriended not long after we moved into our

Chapter 8. Making Friends, Losing Friends

property in the Bonogin Valley, was someone who, despite recognizing his absence, he pursued to a lesser degree. On the last morning we saw the brown pony, Buster made a bee-line for him, overtaking a fellow morning walker in order to get there. As the man walked past, he managed to witness the antics of these two unlikely mates. Buster was rolling around on the ground nuzzling noses with the pony and allowing her to lick his tummy. Watching this, my neighbour said with delight "How cute is that?" In the days and weeks to follow, Buster would stop by on the other side of the road to check just in case the pony was there, but with nowhere near the persistence he had with Rocco.

Of all the dogs he befriended over the course of his life, Didi was, without doubt, his closest companion. AKA 'Devil', Didi was a blue heeler who lived on the first property around the corner from us in Bonogin and they spent many an hour together playing, swimming, going for walks in the Valley or just hanging out in each other's presence, usually while their mums caught up for a cuppa, or at times purely off their own bat! Whilst Didi was a little older than Buster and their temperaments slightly different, what made them great mates was that they were the most equal in size and intelligence of the dogs he met. Interestingly, this feeling of equality is what makes for good friends and partners in people too! With Buster and Didi noticeably older and less frisky by the time we left the Valley, I was sad to see them being separated from one another when we moved to Carrara where our opportunities to catch up would become few and far between. Now both in Spirit, I like to think they're playing together in the skies and enjoying one another's company once more.

Heading out for a swim in the local waterhole with his best mate Didi, in the back of a Holden HZ Ute – can't get much more Australian than that!

Chapter 8. Making Friends, Losing Friends

As kids grow into adolescents and beyond, we find that we often know less about who their friends are and what they get up to when they're not around us. In his last home, Buster had the good fortune to be surrounded by a number of other dogs with whom he could connect. While he knew the dogs on all three sides of our backyard and was always observant of the goings-on in the neighbourhood through the front fence, his favourite was the dog on the other side of the fence at the top of our rather steep backyard. Most often, when I couldn't find him, Buster would be sitting having a 'chat' with his neighbour through the fence palings looking pretty chuffed with himself and it seemed he could sit there for some time just enjoying being in the proximity of his buddy. Once upon a time in Australia the chat over the back fence was a fairly common event and one way we remained connected to those in our community, built relationships with our neighbours and no doubt indulged in the occasional gossip – all harmless of course! This was vital to our wellbeing and built what is referred to as Social Capital, of which, it would appear, there are now comparatively fewer stocks in abundance.

Initially unaware of the change in his behaviour, as time passed, I recall noticing with some sadness that Buster had not ventured up to visit his friend for a little while, no doubt because of the difficulty of navigating the more rugged terrain. I wonder if they missed one another during this time. Nonetheless, the day after he passed, we heard the unmistakable sound of the neighbour's dogs crying and knew that they too were feeling the loss. As in all things, our friendships are subject to the Cycle of Life, the birth, death and rebirth that is part of our existence on planet Earth and I imagine throughout the Universe and it warrants our acknowledgement and respect.

Chapter 9.
The Gentle Art of Persuasion

'The most important persuasion tool you have in your entire arsenal is your integrity.'

Zig Ziglar

Life has been referred to as a game by many a revered sage throughout time. A vast collection of work has been devoted to teaching people how to successfully invite others to play with them on whatever field they are engaged. In the inspirational 1989 movie 'Field of Dreams', Kevin Costner is challenged to breaking point to have faith in what might appear to be an impossible dream. And yet, with persistence, a great deal of hard work and unrelenting faith, what was impossible becomes true-to-life, bringing to him a steady stream of players and rewards to his game and his life. What is so refreshing and encouraging in this story are the words "Build it and they will come", which became the mantra for many in pursuit of their dreams. Not without its challenges, misfortune or heartache, there is something about this that can be seen as a spiritual approach to life and success. So many virtues – like surrender, humility, willingness and patience – are peppered throughout this story and integral to its teachings. Above all, apart from an invincible belief in oneself and one's dreams, there is no force, no heavy-handed sales or attempts to manipulate someone to make choices that are not of their own free will. In what may be seen as 'The Gentle Art of Persuasion', Buster too was a Master.

In most households, early mornings are typically busy times and prone to things going unnoticed. Once he began sleeping in the garage in Bonogin, we were mindful of letting Buster go outside as soon as possible for his morning ablutions, after which he'd usually return to share the morning with Roberto and myself. At some point it dawned on me that he was taking quite a long time to come back inside and I became somewhat curious to find out what was consuming his attention. By this time, we had extended his playground so that he could run all the way down to the boundary of Roberto's workshop and he

Chapter 9. The Gentle Art of Persuasion

spent many a joyous time sprinting and barking at cars as they drove past our property. What I was completely unaware of was just exactly what he **was** up to on those early mornings.

To ensure I didn't disturb him, I tip-toed out to the back door to find him being totally spoilt by one of our neighbours who had stopped to play with him as, I was soon to discover, she had been doing for some time. What made this so, so sweet was that she wasn't just out having a morning walk on her own, but was actually taking both her horse and her own dog for a walk as well. As I stood in the doorway, I watched with amazement as she dismounted her horse and held on to its reins and her dog with one hand, while she reached her other hand through the fence to pick up Buster's rubber toy, Cuz. Deftly she would then slide it up through the gaps in the fencing to the top and then throw it into the yard for Buster to chase. Apart from the skill it would have taken to do that, I was totally blown away – and secretly delighted – that Buster's charms had so successfully enticed her cooperation. Clearly, he had offered her an invitation to play that she could not resist! And no, she was not the only one who stopped to play with Buster from outside the fence and always, whether it was man or woman, girl or boy, it appeared that the joy of engagement was a mutually satisfying one.

Buster was never afraid to ask for what he wanted and his reward was overwhelmingly to receive it. Perhaps he'd read the biblical saying, 'Ask and it shall be given, seek and ye shall find.' In the end, we all just want to have fun and I'm sure had he had a middle name, there would have been none more fitting for Buster than 'fun'!

Chapter 10. Personal Power

'Great is only he, who feels equal to others, because the greatest that we have is that which we share (or have in common) with all people. He who feels and acknowledges this greatness in himself, knows he is great and at the same time feels connected with all other people. If he acknowledges this for himself, at the same time he acknowledges it in all other people and he knows he is equal to all.'

Bert Hellinger

Being a staffy x kelpie breed, Buster was a medium-sized dog weighing in, once full-grown, at around 17-19 kg and standing no taller than my knees. The grassed area that ran alongside the creek across the road from us was the site of one of our early morning walks, particularly when I was short of time. Most of the houses that backed on to this land had a dog or two; in one lived a smaller breed of dog who shared his home with a large, very easy-going Labrador. Whenever we approached this home, the little dog would come running toward us full pelt. Everything about his demeanour was unfriendly and the vibration of fear emanating from him was palpable. Effortlessly, he would shimmy under the fence to escape the yard and pursue us with hackles raised, barking in a loud, high-pitched yap. Annoyed, I would tell him to be quiet and stop disturbing the peace of our morning walks. After a while, seeing the fruitlessness of this, I would instead offer this critter words of comfort like, "It's okay, no one is going to hurt you."

What I loved was Buster's response to all this commotion. Or more accurately, his lack of response! Undaunted, Buster would continue his morning frolic; chasing lizards as they raced toward the shelter of the creek, or, in spite of my disgust, stopping to roll on something whose pungent aroma had caught his attention and rarely even so much as gave a side glance to the other dog. It was as if to say, "What's all the fuss about? I know who I am and there's nothing I have to prove." For the most part we could handle it, but when passing by the front of his house the dog would come out barring his teeth and going for Buster's heels, the

Chapter 10. Personal Power

protector in me would come out in full force. On the morning this occurred, I discovered from a neighbour that there was no person or animal this dog did not greet in like fashion.

While some would label this small dog syndrome, his behaviour was not unlike that of humans who, lacking a feeling of personal power, seek to have power over others through bullying and harassment. All the anger and aggression, all the wasted energy to protect his territory or prove how tough he was; none of it was necessary, for we were no threat to him or his safety. Without ever having been told to, Buster demonstrated with equanimity the ability to ignore and found no need to bark back or retaliate.

On the other hand, Buster also knew his place in the hierarchy and always showed humility in the company of larger dogs by placing himself lower than them or lying at their feet. As I reflect upon this, it appears we humans have lost sight of that pecking order. Whether you call it respect or simply recognition, we lose something fundamental to our collective identity when we fail to pay homage to those who are older, wiser, or more experienced. In our rush to prove ourselves or make it to the top, we sometimes forget to honour our mentors or those who have come before us and learn from the path they have travelled. Accepting our differences, as well as our similarities and respecting individuality, means we are all free to stand in our own power and there is no need to compare ourselves with others or loss of face in 'allowing' another to be who they are or to celebrate their success. Ultimately, the permission to be ourselves is our responsibility ... and at times it is also clear that some people resist others being who they are or put obstacles in their way, by the things that they say and do, to or about them.

Chapter 11. Buster the Swimming Champ

> *'It's a beautiful thing, diving into the cool crisp water and then just being able to sort of pull your body through the water and the water opening up for you.'*
>
> **Dawn Fraser**

Buster was a natural in the water and, given the places where we lived, fortunate to always be in the vicinity of both still water and the ocean. Of them all, it was in Bonogin that Buster was never more than a short walk – or run –- to a natural swimming hole. Bonogin Creek ran the length of the Valley and following heavy rains we were fortunate that, from the top of our property, we could hear it gurgling over the rocks as it passed by below. Apart from having his very own stretch of the Creek to play in, there were a number of places where it meandered on either side of and beneath the main road, where Buster could enjoy an early morning dip. While he was definitely spoilt for choice, he rarely passed up the chance to swim in his favourite water hole, where he would scramble down the rocks and swim to his heart's content.

Buster's Favourite Waterhole – Bonogin Valley

The Valley was known to be a reserve where the endangered glossy black cockatoo could seek shelter and feed from the casuarina trees that still abound there. One morning that remains etched in my mind, we had just arrived at Buster's swimming

Chapter 11. Buster the Swimming Champ

hole when in flew a number of glossy blacks. Just breaking the silence, the sound of their wings softly flapping in the breeze and their unmistakable call was all that preceded their coming in to view. Watching them through the mist of the cold early dawn was almost a spiritual experience, as if we were in the presence of something sacred and unique, which no doubt we were. Even as he swam, Buster remained quiet so as not to disturb the sanctity of this precious moment; the whole event a privilege to witness. Whether it was reverence or not, Buster demonstrated the same quiet presence some years later when, in Maudsland, we were blessed to be visited by an equally mystical creature in the form of a tawny frog mouth perched atop our clothes line.

Given that we were living in a semi-rural area, I wanted Buster to make the most of our morning outings, so our routine was that he would walk 'free-range' going out, doing the things that dogs do and on the return journey, I would put him on his leash so that we could be attached and he knew that we were on our way back home. As I leant down to secure his leash, I would seize the opportunity to give him a kiss on the forehead, a morning ritual that expressed my love for him and which he accepted without visible signs of embarrassment long after he went through puberty and beyond.

Like most kids when it comes to play, Buster really loved to push the envelope and would often test me to see how serious I was when I said it was time to go home. On the opposite side of the road from his water hole was another area where he loved to swim. Whenever he was feeling frisky, he would no sooner have climbed up the embankment on one side (something his Kelpie breed could do with ease) than he'd run across the road – with my permission – and commence swimming in the creek on the other side. It was rare that he had to share this pool with other dogs so this was a blissful experience for him. However, unlike Buster, the time available to me was finite and I would remind him that Mummy had things to do and we were on a time-line. So, I introduced a routine whereby, when it was time to go, I would pick up his leash and walk to the edge of the pool and say goodbye. I'll never forget the first time he saw me do that. He jumped out of the water, stood at the edge and stared at me as if to see if I meant business or not, and once it was clear that I did, ran full pelt to meet me and commence our journey back home together.

As he walked home beside me on his leash, he would follow the white line at the side of the road, stopping every so often to shake the water from his body – which I would gleefully mimic – before we continued onward. One morning, having only

Chapter 11. Buster the Swimming Champ

recently watched the movie of the same name, I laughed when I heard myself say, "Go on Buster, Walk the Line." He was so dependable that I would often just close my eyes and walk home allowing the sun to warm my face as he followed the white line, opening them only when I heard the sound of a car or passer-by, or sensed we had neared our destination.

Whenever he swam in still waters, such as Pizzey Park, the site of many a Sunday morning swim in our years at Bonogin and Carrara, Buster would make the most of his swimming prowess, forging his way through the water unperturbed by ducks and other water life, focused solely on swimming as far as he could before being called back or to retrieve a stick we had thrown for him. If either of us was swimming with him, we would usually wear a rashie to protect ourselves from his nails as he swam torpedo-like straight for – and sometimes over the top of – us. The speed with which he swam was amazing and I would sometimes be hard-pressed to get a swim in without him catching up to me and igniting fits of laughter. Never one to let us rest on our laurels, Buster was always surprising us with some new antic. By far the funniest thing he ever did was the day of his first family swim at our new swimming hole at Bel Air Park, Mermaid Waters, a man-made lake with views out to the Hinterland that we discovered only in our last years at Carrara. My sister-in-law, Elena, was visiting from Italy at the time and captured this on video. Clearly enjoying himself, when we decided it was time to go, I lifted Buster out of the water and to our delight his little legs just kept on swimming, like an air-guitar player's arms, no water but plenty of paddle!

Surfing the waves at Miami Beach

Like his mum and dad, the beach was one of Buster's favourite places to be. He would run and play, roll in the sand and uncover treasures, jump into the ocean and surf the waves or sit on the sand checking out the view, keeping an ever-watchful eye out for anyone who needed 'rescuing'. If he saw someone out on a surfboard – which

Chapter 11. Buster the Swimming Champ

unsurprisingly there were a few to say the least – it would take either all our strength to hold him back or lots of comforting to let him know they were, indeed, okay without his help. Less attached to swimming than I, invariably Roberto would either take Buster for a walk to divert his attention or hold onto him with the tightest of reins while I went in for a dip myself. Even up until his very last swim, Buster would not allow me to go into the water unless he gave it his best shot to go in after me, yet another indication of the beautiful spirit of this precious little guy.

Chapter 12. Buster's Run | Forging Pathways of Change

'In any given moment we have two options: to step forward into growth or to step back into safety.'

Abraham Maslow

Until very recent times in our history, we believed that human beings were incapable of change; that a leopard doesn't change his spots, or that we are at the mercy of our genes. People of my parents' generation were referred to as the 'Generation of No Change' and the 'Silent Generation' and on reflection, I see how the two went together and were designed to keep us loyal to the status quo. For how do we bring about change, particularly in the things that cause us discomfort, if we don't even talk about them? We thought that the brain itself was hardwired and we were doomed to remain stuck in our patterns of thought, feeling and behaviour and, for all but the most adventurous, that was how we lived our lives. "That's just the way I am." or "He is just like that." were the catch-cries and justifications for why things remained the same. It was the perfect combination for perpetuating misery and keeping people frozen and stuck in pain, belonging to an era that has since proven to be incongruent with those who would seek to be self-actualised and fulfil their own destiny rather than one dictated to them.

With breakthroughs in brain research by pioneers like Norman Doidge MD, we now understand that the brain can change, we can choose to do something different and, as we do, we literally alter the neural pathways that had heretofore been considered fixed and permanent. When explaining this to my clients to help them understand the process of change, I often use the story of Buster's Run as a teaching metaphor.

As I've said, dogs are creatures of habit. Consequently, they like to keep things simple and prefer not to expend any unnecessary energy. So, it stands to reason that when they want to get from point A to point B, they're most likely going to follow the same route each time. And so, in

Bonogin, that's exactly what Buster did! Running in his enclosed area each day in the same direction, he eventually forged a path in the grass that I referred to as 'Buster's Run'. The more he used it, the more the grass beneath it died and the easier it became to run along the same track. In our terms, this is equivalent to our comfort zone or the unconscious, automatic, well-worn actions and reactions we have to life. As one Family Constellations Workshop participant identified, we become used to our 'uncomfortable Comfort Zones', whether they serve us or not. To break the patterns that have held us back, we must learn how to do something we haven't done before – to do what initially is uncomfortable – but eventually leads to growth and change.

At some point we decided to erect fencing along the border of the grassed area beside the driveway for Roberto's workshop. This allowed us to open the gate that had previously marked the boundary of Buster's play area and gave him more use of the property where we lived. It was at this time that he began to run in the opposite direction to his original run and it wasn't long before a new pathway began to emerge. At the same time, as his trips down that first path dwindled and it was given less attention, the grass began to grow once more and before too long the path itself had all but disappeared.

Chapter 12. Buster's Run | Forging Pathways of Change

Where he had been accustomed to running in one direction, his default was now to take the new road travelling in the opposite direction, making it the new 'Buster's Run'.

In the same way, when we are in the process of change, it's likely that for a time we will be drawn back to the old way; that it will take a little while and greater conscious attention to practice and strengthen new behaviours before they become automatic. As we do, just like the grass that was left to renew itself in Buster's playground, the old neural pathways will recede, giving precedence to new neural pathways and allowing a new way of being or doing to become our default, with the freedom that accompanies that.

Chapter 13. I Won't Let You Forget (Me)

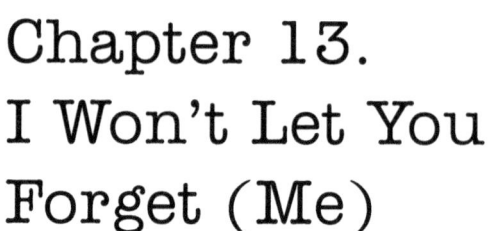

> 'We need 4 hugs a day for survival. We need 8 hugs a day for maintenance. We need 12 hugs a day for growth.'
>
> **Virginia Satir**

Whether we like it or not, there are some things we just never fully get over or let go of without a little help. Even though it makes me laugh when I think of the way he did it, Buster's choice to abstain from drinking water when we were out, had its roots in one of life's biggest traumas; being abandoned as a baby or a helpless child.

From the first moment we laid eyes on him until his own had closed, our sacred contract was to be there for Buster, to not leave him alone or abandon

Chapter 13. I Won't Let You Forget (Me)

him as had been his early life experience. While he came from a litter of eight, we will never know how young he was when he was torn from his mother, or how long he had been without his brothers and sisters at the RSPCA before we arrived to claim him as our own. There was something so primal about this little being. It made us and our friends not want him to ever experience anything other than knowing that he was loved and treasured absolutely. I am so sure that even if we had also been the parents of human children, he would still have elicited that love and devotion because of who he was. I know as I write this that it sounds a little like I am idolising Buster ... and for the moment, I am okay with that!

At some point, when I was really struggling to earn a living and feeling somewhat isolated living in the Bonogin Valley, it became apparent to me that I had made the decision to keep working from home and not venture out, as Roberto had repeatedly encouraged me to do, in order to be there for Buster. I don't recall if that realisation became the catalyst for me to step out of my comfort zone, or because at the time I was collaborating with Family Lawyers in the city and wanted to be closer to them for the clients we were working with as a team. Motivated to break out of my rut, I seized the opportunity to find myself a venue where I could see clients in

Brisbane once a week, build my practice up again and just get out of the house and be among other human beings. So, I found myself a beautiful clinic in Hawthorne, on the south side of Brisbane and set myself up to begin consulting there. Usually this meant I would leave home around 5:30 or 6:00 am and return somewhere between 9:00-10:00 pm, a whole new experience for me and for Buster!

On the afternoon of my first day working at Urban Retreat, Roberto arrived home to find that Buster had not had a drink of water since he had left for work that morning. In the heat of summer, this was not an ideal scenario! From that day on, whenever we were away for more than an hour or so, when we arrived home, the first thing Buster would do after greeting us would be to go to his water bowl and drink for a full minute or two. Watching his tongue lapping up the water through the glass of his favourite drinking bowl until his thirst was quenched, I marvelled at his determination to uphold his protest. This was his way to let us know his displeasure with being left alone, and despite our reminders to him to drink while we were away, he continued to guilt us throughout the rest of his life with this very effective tactic. This both upset and astounded us; that he could still be fretting when we left him after so many years of consistently returning home to him, or

Chapter 13. I Won't Let You Forget (Me)

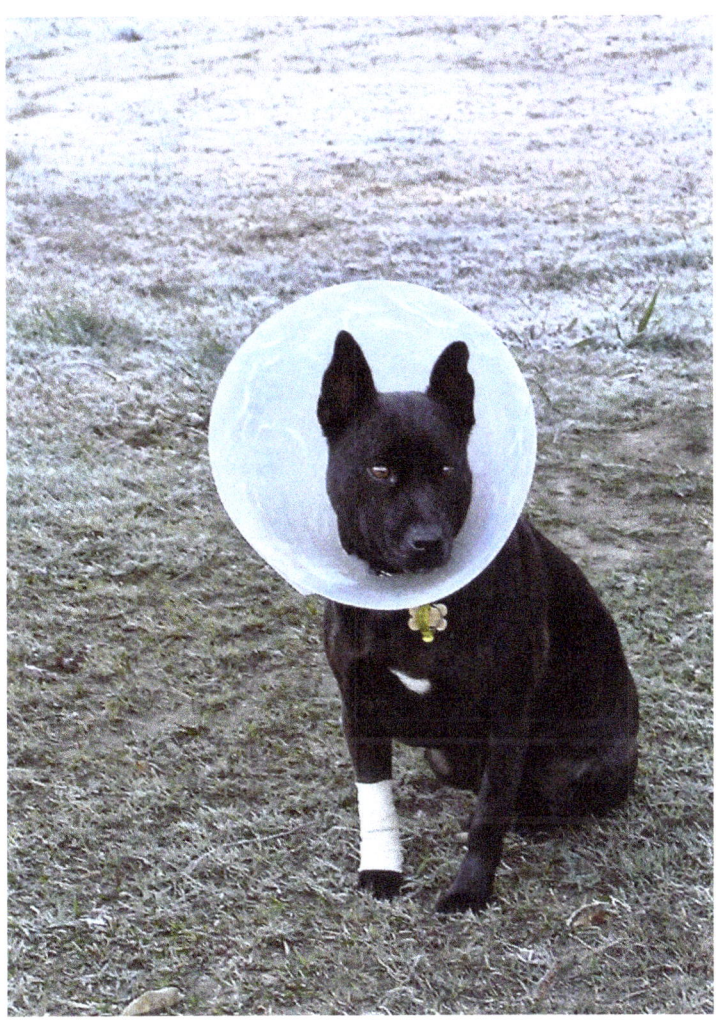

Now how could you ever forget him? Even with his collar and wound he insisted on playing with his Cuz (toy in top left corner) on a cold and frosty morning. Irresistible!

that he could actually last that long without water when it was in bowls all around the yard! Despite all this and much to our surprise and relief, his active resistance had zero effect on his kidneys, which remained healthy and strong until the end. One time when I was away in Sydney for work and Buster was doing his usual thing at home, I recall saying to my mother that I thought I'd raised him to be independent of me. In reply, she jokingly suggested that, perhaps, on that count, I had 'failed'. Point taken! Yet another reminder that we are never gonna get it all right as parents!

Despite this behaviour, Buster always greeted us with wild effervescence, running in circles and yelping his welcoming barks when we walked in the door: something of which I would never, ever have tired. Imagine if our partners and children were to greet us in that manner or we were to welcome them home with the same enthusiasm and joy? Licks aside, a whole lot more love and appreciation would be flowing at home if that were the case! Not that Buster had to be glued to our sides all the time either. When we were at home or he was staying with others, once he knew people were around, he would happily play outside or lie in the sun or his kennel on his own. Similarly, once children have the security of knowing they can trust and depend on us, that we are there for them no matter what – a critical element of keeping them

Chapter 13. I Won't Let You Forget (Me)

safe when they start experimenting with risky behaviours – they can step out and explore life and all it holds for them. Knowing that when they need to, they can return for connection, comfort, advice and sustenance, helps them to grow into healthy young people able to make their way in the world, which, I believe, is every parent's wish come true.

Chapter 14. All is Right in the World Again

'Every child comes with the message that God is not yet discouraged of man.'

Rabindranath Tagore

Just as Pavlov's dog learned to salivate at the sound of the bell that signalled the coming of mealtime, Buster also developed a conditioned response to a bell's ring. Every second Sunday morning in Bonogin the ice-cream van would pull in to the bottom of our street on the other side of our property and wait until it was a respectable time before ringing his bell to alert the residents he had arrived. Being 10 kilometres from the nearest shops, this was a service that many appreciated to ensure that their ice cream

Chapter 14. All is Right in the World Again

didn't melt on the way home, especially during the summer months.

It didn't take long for Buster to develop a love for this fortnightly activity, but it wasn't the ice cream that attracted him, but rather the belly-rubs and attention that he would receive from the vendor, whom we affectionately called Uncle Malcolm. Given that he actually had an Uncle Malcolm, my brother in Sydney, it seemed appropriate that he should be known by that name. Once Buster was in sync with his roster, he would pre-empt Uncle Malcolm's arrival, sitting in the yard waiting patiently for him to arrive. As soon as he heard the van turn the corner and park, he would start barking and running excitedly all around the yard, racing down to the border of his enclosure in anticipation. Even without ringing his bell, Buster knew that Malcolm was there and that he would soon have the stimulus of both the bell and its owner with which to connect. Fortunately, living in the Hinterland, our neighbours never complained about being woken by Buster's barking before 8:00 am on a Sunday morning (or if they did, we were none the wiser).

Depending on how many people were interested in purchasing ice cream, Buster would have to wait until Malcolm had served the side street before pulling in to the property directly across from ours. Then, observing the road rules, we would make our way across the road just as Uncle Malcolm would alight from the van in time to meet his biggest fan who would greet him with joyous fervour. These were such memorable and funny times and we were always appreciative of the love Buster exchanged with this warm, kind-hearted man.

Like all folk, there came a time when Uncle Malcolm took a holiday and for a short while, Buster's expectations remained unfulfilled when the van failed to arrive. While it may have given us a brief time to modify our sugar intake, the morning the ice-cream van returned was a momentous day in the Viola household! It just so happened that this coincided with a time when I too had returned home after being away for work for a few days. The first I knew of the good news was when Buster raced into the ensuite, which I was busy cleaning, with his tail wagging feverishly. As I followed him outside to find out what he was so excited about, it became apparent that, at last Uncle Malcom was back! Yay! I called out to Roberto to let him know and then, together, we waited patiently for the van to come up the hill before reconnecting with this precious figure in our lives with Buster, as always, trembling with excitement. On that day Buster did not leave my side for some time afterward and the sense he conveyed was the relief that comes, when finally, we can relax and

Chapter 14. All is Right in the World Again

know that all is right in the world once more. Not only was Mum back, but so too was his special friend and the clanging bell whose sound he obviously enjoyed.

Like so many other people in his life, Buster was loved by Uncle Malcolm and we were all sad when the time came to move out of the Valley and find a new ice-cream man, but not before we secured a lovely snapshot of them doing what they had always done on those early Sunday mornings.

When we moved to Carrara, Buster would bark and run downstairs to see the new ice-cream man, who was friendly but far less affectionate than Uncle Malcolm. Unfortunately, in his last home, because of his hearing loss, he rarely heard the sound of the van in the street and we never became customers of the new vendor. I wish I could say it helped to keep our waistlines in check, but sadly that wasn't the case.

Navigating life's challenges …

Stage Three
Adulthood & Independence

Carrara | Central Gold Coast | QLD

October 2009-December 2016

photo courtesy Elena Viola

Chapter 15. Lessons in Compassion

'The fruit of love is service, which is compassion in action.'

Mother Teresa

From his youngest days, hanging the clothes on the line signified a game to Buster. No sooner would we take the washing basket outside than he would go in search of his rubber toy and drop it at our feet to throw for him as we pegged out the washing. There's no doubt this made it both a more enjoyable and more time-consuming task for Roberto and myself! There were a few things about this that were lessons for me.

The first, that a half-hearted approach to play – when you're doing two things at once – often carries with it a penalty; in this case, of having the toy land in a tree rather than somewhere Buster could easily retrieve it. This attempt to save time invariably cost me time as I found myself climbing trees or grabbing brooms to pry toys out from between branches after my less-than-well-directed throw landed them in some place inaccessible to Buster. The first time this happened, I realised just how important it was that his toy be found and returned to him. Like any child who has lost something they love, he would not leave the base of the tree (or stop barking) until I located it and it was once more available to play with. This was when I first understood how the meaning of compassion – to suffer with – applied to Buster. If he had momentarily lost his toy, then it was my job to suffer the consequences of my poorly projected throw and do for him what it was that he could not. To even consider not doing that seemed cruel and inconsiderate toward an animal whose nature it is to live in the moment, let alone ignorant to and disrespectful of his needs. Seeing that ball or toy stuck in a tree or drain was clearly painful to him and it was only once it was returned that he, and I, could both be at ease again.

Oddly enough, when we left Bonogin, to move into our first home on the Gold Coast proper, for a short while it escaped our attention that something was missing. For whatever reason, the previous owners had hung all their washing indoors and for some time, while it was still

Chapter 15. Lessons in Compassion

convenient for us, we did the same. It wasn't until we erected an outdoor clothes line and first began to hang our washing there that Buster reminded us of the game we had failed to recognise had been missing from his repertoire of play. It's said that elephants never forget and I think the same could be said of dogs, at least in Buster's case. As soon as that clothes line was put to use he was at our feet throwing his toy down to play the game again! It was only when he did this that we actually remembered that this had been our routine in the past.

This was another lesson that, like Buster, our children remember; our promises, the things we said we would do or give to them, as well as the promises we do not keep or the times we failed to notice what was important to them or that they were in pain. Sometimes it may be the most insignificant thing to us that will, in fact, matter most to a child or stranger and an act of love which respects that and responds accordingly. Long before our children can speak, they feel and those feelings are either acknowledged and respected or not, providing the template from which they will learn how to treat themselves and others in the future.

Often when we are called upon to be compassionate it may not necessarily be comfortable or timely for us. However, with willingness, loving intent, and patience, the rewards of doing so far surpass the time and effort involved. Just one of countless opportunities to practice loving kindness, this was one of many examples of how Buster inspired and deepened my understanding of compassion. Apart from the rare occasion when I was certain that he had called me "Mum" or made those garbled noises that represent a dog talking, there were so many other ways in which he communicated his needs and wants, as well as his appreciation for having them met.

Chapter 16. Time-Out for Fun!

'Play is the highest form of research.'

Albert Einstein

If there was one lesson Buster taught me above all others, it was the necessity of play and the importance of having fun.

Being with Buster, as it had with children, gave me permission to have fun, be silly, and to do the things which gave me joy. One of my fondest memories in my life before Buster came along, was the day I was playing on the trampoline with our friend's daughter Aria, then just 4 years old. I was having a great time when, in her wisdom, looking at me rather earnestly, she proclaimed, "Di, you need some kids!" How right she was! Whilst walking and swimming and fetch were a regular pastime with Buster, I was yet to discover that he and I would share yet another love I had from my own distant childhood.

Selfie on a Swing!

Walking through the park across the road from our home in Carrara one morning, I realised for the first time that there was also a children's playground there, modestly fitted out with a swing and other equipment. As I opened the gate to go inside and test out the swing to see if it would accommodate my size and weight, it occurred to me to invite Buster to join me. To my delight, when I picked him up and put him on my lap he sat there contentedly as I pushed the swing back-and-forth with my feet. While I kept it pretty low-key, abstaining from doing

Chapter 16. Time-Out for Fun!

any of those round the world turns we attempted as kids, he stayed just long enough for us both to enjoy the freedom of being on a swing before wriggling out of my arms to return to solid ground.

Thereafter, each time we would approach the playground, even before I asked if he wanted to have a swing, he would stop outside the gate and wait for permission to enter the enclosure. Once he'd had his turn on the swing with me, he would sit happily on the sand while I had a more vigorous turn by myself. Capturing this with selfies and video remain some of my most treasured memories of my boy. And while I am certain it was not exactly kosher to take a dog in there, there were never any other children or adults in sight, and he was always respectful and left no unwelcome 'surprises'.

Allowing ourselves to enjoy pleasurable experiences such as these enrich our lives and nourish our souls. Children and animals know that life is meant to be a game and will always seek out others to join them. In our ever-quickening lives, taking – or making – the time to do this has become not only more difficult, but ever more critical to our physical, emotional, mental and spiritual wellbeing. Even when we know this, many of us still struggle to prioritise it, or make having fun conditional upon completing all the other things we 'have to do' first and so, life becomes a waiting game! Whilst we will always have responsibilities to attend to, balancing work with play is essential if we are to avoid feeling shallow and unfulfilled.

One of the ways I caught myself doing this was when I would tell Buster that I didn't have time to take him for a walk in the morning and we'd go at night instead, words he would never allow me to forget! He'd go about his normal business throughout the day then at some point he'd let me know that I hadn't yet kept my promise. And that would colour everything I did until finally I made the conscious choice to act on that promise and do what I had said I would. In part, it had to do with the benefit of the experience itself. Taking Buster for a walk was something that enriched both our lives. The other aspect of it is best expressed in the words of Khalil Gibran who says, "Oftentimes in denying yourself pleasure you do but store the desire in the recesses of your being."

Whether it's the head space it takes up, or the time we waste thinking and worrying about whether or not to do it, the energy it takes to actually do something is usually far less than the energy of holding ourselves back from it.

Knowing I'd withheld from myself the simple pleasure, not to mention benefits, of having my morning walk would, more often than not, actually restrict my ability or effectiveness in achieving the

Chapter 16. Time-Out for Fun!

very things I had deemed as more important. My default, learnt as a child, was to put work before play and this was not easily shifted within me. I have since learnt that 'bringing a sense of playfulness into the whole of life, notwithstanding the need for reverence on occasion, seems a goal worth pursuing'[1]. And yet, in many ways, reverence and playfulness can go hand in hand. I observed this in the behaviour of the Dalai Lama at the 'Happiness & Its Causes Conference' in Sydney some years ago where, even in the hot seat on stage, he would bring a lightness to his presentation and interactions with others, remaining on task, while at the same time having fun and eliciting humour in both the panel and the audience.

Without exception, every time I honoured my word and took Buster for a walk or an outing, I would return home happy that I had done it even when it meant putting something else aside. With my love for Buster as my motivation – as well as the peace he would give me once it was done – to this day I am grateful for every single time I downed tools and just went out to play!

---

(1) To read more about the benefits of play, please see my article on 'Playfulness' on my website www.positiverelating.com

Chapter 17.
Up for the Challenge

'Only children believe they are capable of everything.'

Paulo Coelho

One of the most captivating things about Buster was his lack of awareness of any limits. As a puppy he stood no taller than knee-high-to-a-grasshopper, with such tiny little legs and yet, when given a bone almost as big as he, he would run around the backyard with it in his mouth before taking refuge beneath a tree to eat it. We were soon discouraged from giving him these for the potential they had to cause him tummy problems due to their high fat content.

However, the bones were no match for the sticks he would find on our morning walks. People we met would marvel at his strength as they

Chapter 17. Up for the Challenge

ducked and weaved to avoid being scratched when Buster ran past them with sticks that were actually the fallen branches of trees. To see him wielding a stick that could be anywhere up to four times the length of his body, and no doubt equally as weighty, was a source of delight and amusement to behold. If the stick was particularly heavy, he'd pick it up between his teeth, run a short distance, plonk it down while he caught his breath and then pick it back up again and run even faster. There were times he clearly expected me to throw them for him as well, which he would indicate by repeatedly spitting them out at my feet in frustration. Of course, I refused, despite his barking protestations.

With the combination of staffy and kelpie, he was both a really strong and agile dog with the ability to run and jump quite high, as he would have done had he been a working dog jumping on the backs of sheep and cattle to keep them in line. I'm not sure if that's where his quirky behaviour during our game of fetch came from or not, but it never ceased to evoke a giggle or two. When we would throw his toy for him at home, he would run and fetch it, then return and drop it our feet ready for the next throw. As he waited he would do a 360-degree turn – anti-clockwise – before running to retrieve his toy again. Perhaps it was his way of unfurling his body or simply just an expression of glee. It was such a delightfully funny thing to watch and we would wait expectantly before throwing his toy to see if he would do it again. While this game was created in part to protect him from over-exerting himself or jumping in ways that could do his body harm, the truth is that had we left it to him – as we inadvertently did on occasion when children would play with him – he would happily have kept going until his heart gave out. So, I instigated two commands that helped us to keep things in perspective. Over time, the actual number of turns decreased in order to accommodate his ageing process, however we always followed the same procedure. When there were just two runs to go, as he approached us we would say, holding up two fingers, "Two more, two more!" and on the final leg, "Last one, last one!", before heading back inside to give him his morning treat.

Whilst Buster never appeared to suffer from feelings of inadequacy, and as much as we adored his spirit, clearly it was up to us to teach him the boundaries that would keep him safe and healthy. Instinctively he could jump from a standing position and leap a 4' high retaining wall, seemingly with ease. However, what that may do to his hips was not something we wanted to find out. Then there were the times he would leave us dumbfounded after finding him happily

Chapter 17. Up for the Challenge

You know those big sticks I was talking about? Well, this wasn't one of them, but Buster still insisted that we play fetch with it!

sitting in the driver's seat of Roberto's van, a feat that required both a twist and a leap from the floor where we'd left him only minutes before. In his little head, he had unlimited potential to run, jump, swim and play and, for the most part, he did just that. We never taught him not to believe in himself and so he would go for it. Again, a moment I am so glad I captured on film, was the day he took one of his sticks into his kennel and then tried to get it out. In the process, the stick got lodged horizontally in the opening of the kennel and try as he might, he was unable to pry it loose. While it made for a delightful snapshot of the expression on his face, this was another of those times when mum or dad needed to show compassion and do for him what he could not.

Chapter 17. Up for the Challenge

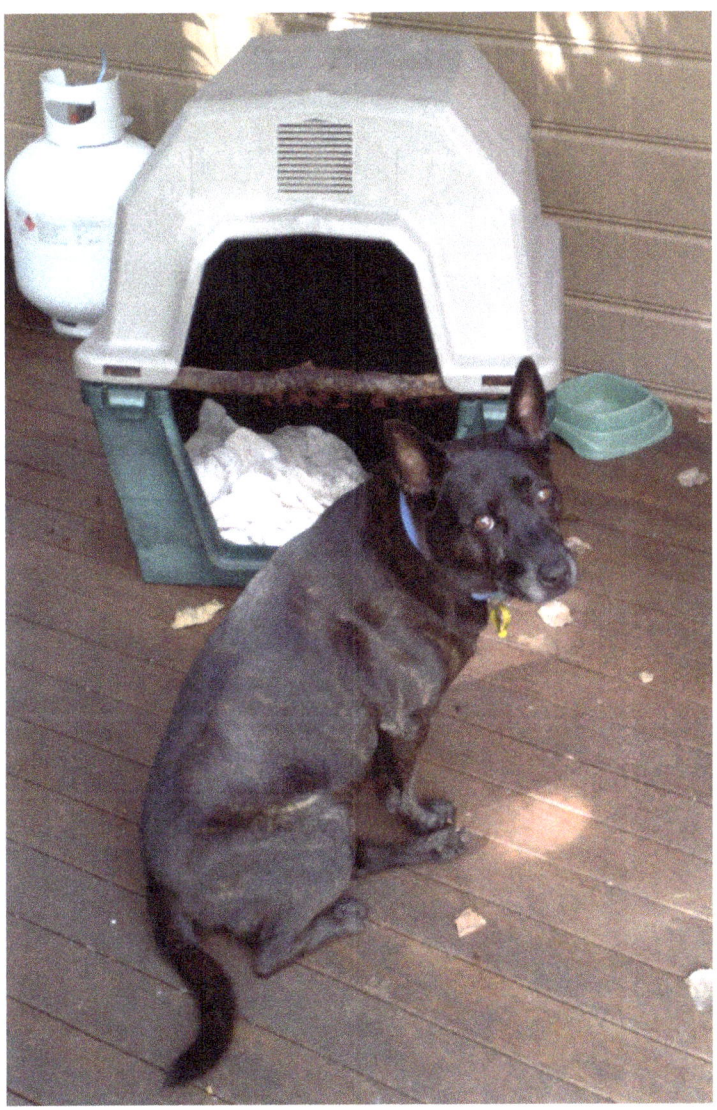

Chapter 18.
My Ears Hurt When You Speak That Way

> *'Most of us grew up speaking a language that encourages us to label, compare, demand, and pronounce judgements rather than to be aware of what we are feeling and needing.'*
>
> **Marshall B. Rosenberg**

The first client I ever shared this story with asked good-humouredly, "Do you think we could rent Buster out for six months?"

Whether we are consciously aware of it or not, we are all constantly picking up on the energy of others. Despite what people might say when asked, "How are you?" the feeling or vibration they exude says more than words ever could. There's no denying what it feels like when you enter a room where

Chapter 18. My Ears Hurt When You Speak That Way

you could cut the air with a knife or alternately, the feeling you get when you walk into a home and know you have to buy it because it feels just right. Everything is energy and E-motion is energy in motion. Unlike humans, dogs have no filter for energy and simply feel or sense exactly what is going on around them.

Being of Lebanese descent and married to an Italian born, you might imagine there would be a few sparks flying around during times of disagreement or conflict in our home. I certainly have the capacity to raise my voice and when I'm not being really conscious, I can be a force to be reckoned with if I don't feel like I'm being heard. I'm not sure when it began, but there came a day when Buster decided it was time to let us know that he didn't like the feeling of what was happening in the house. From that first time onward, whenever Roberto and I were having an argument where it was clear that neither of us was prepared to give up our position, Buster would get up from wherever he was sitting or lying and promptly take himself outside. In no uncertain terms, he would let us know that what we were doing was unacceptable to him!

While at first it took us by surprise, it also very successfully alerted us to what we were doing and reunited us in our desire that Buster be happy and content, even if, for the moment, we were unable to reach an agreement ourselves on what we were arguing about. Far from being a blessing in disguise, his disapproval of our behaviour spoke volumes! So, after saying something like, "See, you upset Buster again!" – a shrewd flick of responsibility to the other – we would call him back into the house and get down on the floor with him to have a family hug. We'd tell him that everything was okay and that Mummy and Daddy still loved him and each other, serving as a reminder to us of that truth as well. By the time we'd done this, whatever we were arguing about had faded into the background and we were brought back to our senses, laughing at the absurdity of it. Buster would then happily resume his place on the floor or his bed and once more be at ease having restored order to the house.

For many people, particularly those raised in a highly conflicted environment, or alternately who had no experience of their parents fighting; avoiding conflict at all costs can become a way of life. While it would be true to say that most people feel some level of discomfort with conflict, it is however part of daily life and learning to 'fight fair' is something we all need to master. Not all conflict is the same and avoidance or resistance does little to change things for the better! Again, while it may not have been immediately apparent to us, there was also a time when we realised that Buster didn't **always** leave the room when we were in conflict. Somehow, when we were working through it and doing our best to resolve whatever the issue was – perhaps with a more open heart and mind – Buster just kept on doing whatever he was doing, unperturbed by our conversation. This in itself became the litmus test to distinguish what we were feeling, where we were at, how committed we were to a peaceful resolution and what we needed to do for ourselves as well as for him.

There's no doubt that living in an environment of tension and conflict is harmful to our emotional, mental and spiritual wellbeing and eventually can also become a source of physical disease, especially if it is consistent or long-term. Buster was able to get up and leave when he needed to because he just followed his nose (AKA his intuition) and did what was right for him. What it does tell us though is that our children, who may be less able to demonstrate their discomfort or disapproval of their parent's behaviour, or who have been witness to it for too long, might simply sit in the energy of it, taking it in and learning that this is the only way to deal with conflict or differences of opinion. There is no doubt that it would be preferable that they had greater choices about this!

Chapter 19. Mind Your Manners

'People of character do the right thing even if no one else does, not because they think it will change the world but because they refuse to be changed by the world.'

Michael Josephson

No book about Buster would be complete without a chapter on just what a well-mannered little being he was. When I think of the words 'mind your manners', it seems they belong to a time long-gone, one where, as children, we were expected to say "please" and "thank you" and to show courtesy, respect and consideration for others. Often such simple things, these social mores were considered integral to the making of a good man or good woman, to someone who could take their place in the world with ease. Many of these were just understood, acquired almost by osmosis by

Chapter 19. Mind Your Manners

virtue of the fact that nearly everyone modelled or reinforced these behaviours. Whether it is stepping aside to allow someone to walk in front of you through a doorway, or to stand up and offer your seat on public transport to someone whose need is greater than yours, these are deliberate acts of kindness that build a more harmonious society which we can ill afford to lose.

There was definitely a sense of pride in seeing Buster employ the simple things we taught him, some by 'accident' and others on purpose. In the canine world, as in the human, there is an order to things and we learned, through taking Buster to Puppy School, the importance of reinforcing those codes of behaviour. Descendants of wolves, our domestic dogs once roamed in packs and the rules they had to function successfully then, remain intrinsic to their behaviour today. Instinctively, they know how things are meant to be and look to the humans in their lives to reinforce that through their behaviour toward and with them. At the same time, just like our human children, they can be impulsive, excitable and full of energy and do not always follow protocol. So, while on occasion we did let things slide, at other times, the reasoning behind what we were doing was patently clear to us. I can still see Buster shimmying from side to side as he waited impatiently at the front door after a family outing, to be the first to race inside the house, pushing past us with no compunction. For the most part, this did not bother us. Then there were other times when we insisted that he sit and wait until Mummy and Daddy had gone through the door before he took his turn, doing our part as parents in reinforcing the orders that help a child to understand his/her place in the world.

From the very beginning, he was taught to shake hands for two reasons: on meeting someone new and before he was given a treat, which he would do from a sitting position, initially with a verbal reminder from us and then later, as a matter of course. It was always so sweet to see him say hello to a small child who would kneel down to meet him face-to-face. Buster would raise his paw to shake hands, to the delight of both child and parents. No doubt there was many a time when he expected a treat to accompany the greeting and he would often make the gesture of another hand shake as his way of letting us know he was ready to receive one, whether it was on offer or not. Like most dogs I'm sure, food was highest on his list of rewards, despite my initial assumption that cuddles came first. No, for Buster the order was food, play and then cuddles.

The one demonstration of manners we never compromised on was his goodnight routine, which embraced all three of those stimuli. Again, I don't

Chapter 19. Mind Your Manners

recall how we came to introduce this, but it gave us many an evening of mirth and remains the memory I would most want to bring back to life, through the Star Wars style holograph I've envisaged one day being possible (at some extraordinary cost, no doubt) from a Hollywood producer. If only! Like so many of his routines, it evolved over time, changing as he changed with age. This was his bedtime schedule. He would either be outside relaxing on the grass under the stars and we would have a last play for the day or hanging out with us in the lounge room on his canvas stretcher. Like all good children, he was required to clean his teeth before he went to bed at night. Crunching on a frozen chicken neck every night for nearly 15 years was anything but a chore for Buster and it kept his teeth and gums in such great condition that he never required any dental treatment, something for which we were all most grateful. I imagine my Aunty Edna, who had reinforced the importance of dental hygiene in my childhood, would have been looking down on us, pleased that her reminders had not fallen on deaf ears and her efforts had been rewarded.

However, before he could receive this last treat for the day, he had to first say goodnight to Mummy and Daddy, just as we would expect any child to do. While initially it was just myself or Roberto that this applied to, on the first occasion that we had house guests, we flippantly insisted, half expecting him not to follow through, that he say goodnight to everyone there, which he obeyed to our amusement and pride. Thereafter, this became the tradition in our home; whoever was present at bedtime would receive a kiss, or more accurately, a lick, on the leg or hand according to their preference, as Buster's way of saying "Goodnight", prior to him bounding back across the lounge to claim his chook neck. Clearly eager to get to the prize, Buster would often make a half-hearted effort to do the first part, going so far but not far enough to actually reach us, before heading back in the direction of the kitchen. Whilst he may have given these short-cuts a couple of attempts, we never let him get away with it, laughing as we insisted that he say goodnight properly before expecting to be given his treat. Such was the joy that he brought to our daily lives!

Chapter 20. Developing Self-Discipline

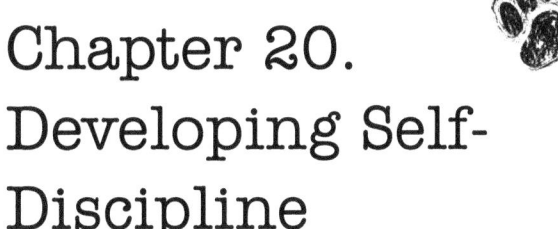

> *'Discipline is the basic set of tools we require to solve life's problems. Without discipline we can solve nothing. With only some discipline we can solve only some problems. With total discipline we can solve all problems.'*
>
> **M. Scott Peck**

As a parent, one of the greatest gifts we can give our children is to inculcate them in self-discipline and the sooner that instruction begins, the better! With the benefit of formal behavioural classes for puppies, from which Buster graduated with flying colours, as well as my own background as a Special Education Teacher, there was much I could bring to the job of raising him. Teaching Buster boundaries, which are the hallmark of discipline and being consistent in those teachings myself from his earliest days, served to keep him safe throughout his life. As I say to my clients, with discipline, comes freedom, and 'Doing what it takes to teach children discipline, which in turn equips them to become self-disciplined, is both the most loving and at times, the most difficult, job a parent will undertake'[2].

So, when we would walk free-rein and there was a need to keep him safe, I would often just say repeatedly, "Stay with Mummy, stay with Mummy." With my index finger pointing to the ground beside me, Buster would walk at my feet right by my side as well as any dog on a leash.

The best test of any teaching comes when we are faced with a situation for which we have not been specifically trained. In education, this is referred to as generalisation, carrying the knowledge learnt in one setting across to other, new and different scenarios. There was no more impressive example of this ability and Buster's intelligence than the day in Bonogin when he was called upon to control his own behaviour and instinctual responses. At the time, I was talking to Lesley, our neighbour, from the other side of the fence, who had stopped to chat while out walking her own dogs. As he always did, Buster was hanging

Chapter 20. Developing Self-Discipline

around while I was trimming hedges just waiting for another opportunity to engage me in a game of fetch, which, in his mind, was the only reason I was there! When Lesley arrived, he ran around the outside of the property to say hello, taking Cuz, his toy, with him. Accepting his invitation to play, Lesley threw his toy for him and to our horror, on the second throw, it landed right in the middle of the road. As a car swerved to avoid it, we both took a deep breath, and, before I could even utter a word, Buster raced to the edge of the grass and stopped himself just shy of the gutter. The sheer relief of seeing him do this was only surpassed by my absolute pride in Buster for demonstrating such extraordinary self-control. As Lesley and I both let out a nervous laugh, inwardly I vowed never to risk that happening again!

That he had made the distinction to go to the edge and no further undoubtedly saved his life that day and he continued to demonstrate the same judgement in the years when we would play in the front yard in Carrara, which had no actual physical boundary. Whenever a toy bounced onto the road, he would go only so far as the gutter, almost teetering over the edge. If he couldn't reach it from there with his mouth, he would leave it until I or whoever was with him would come to retrieve it on his behalf.

Similarly, he was taught while still a puppy on a leash that we didn't cross the road until I said in a very deep, almost guttural voice, "Go!" at which point we would both walk briskly across the road, stopping only in the middle momentarily where there was a nature strip before the next "Go!" signalled it was time to continue. At other times, when he was off-leash, people would often comment on the way he would wait at the kerb for me to catch up and how confident I was that he would stay until I gave the all-clear. How fortunate I was to be able to trust him to stay safe was brought home to me on more than one occasion when others in our neighbourhood suffered the agony of losing their dogs when they had been hit by cars after running onto the road unsupervised.

Whether it was this training or the 'Puppy Angels' I had instructed him to keep with him, or simply because everyone was still snuggled up in bed at the time, I am so grateful that on the odd occasion that he did go walkabout in Carrara, possibly tired of waiting for me to take him or in pursuit of a friend, that he returned unscathed from his early morning ramblings. While it was only a couple of times, running up the hill in the wee hours of the morning to hunt him down was not something myself or Roberto wanted to

Chapter 20. Developing Self-Discipline

become a habit, let alone to have the experience of anything more dangerous happening to him.

---

(2) To read more about Loving Discipline, please see my article 'Discipline = Love in Action' on my website www.positiverelating.com

Chapter 21. Attention Absolute

> *'The Master gives himself up to whatever the moment brings.'*
>
> **Lao Tzu**

Buster just did exactly what he needed to! Whether it was instinctual or learnt, he remains such a powerful example of a life well-lived. When he played, it was full-out for whatever his body was up for at the time. When he rested, it was also 100%. Buster, it appeared to me, was always only ever in one place at a time; exactly where he was. And yes, it could change in an instant! The sleeping dog could be up and running full-force if something new captured his attention, but for the time that he was resting or eating or drinking or playing, that was the only thing he was focused on. His attention was absolute! His love was also absolute! There was no ambiguity or confusion or

Chapter 21. Attention Absolute

uncertainty. If he was given a treat, which we did religiously before ever leaving him, and he wasn't hungry or ready to eat it at that time, he would take it and bury it somewhere and dig it back up again when his appetite beckoned.

One of the things I found funniest about him was when we would give him a bone or frozen treat and he would look at us and wait for us to go away. It was as if to say he didn't want us to see where he was going to bury it! Roberto and I would often laugh about that, given we were the ones who had offered it to him and it was highly unlikely we were going to go in search of it to eat ourselves. I wonder if that was instinctual; what any dog in the wild would do to ensure his predators or other dogs didn't steal it out from under his nose. And did he think of Roberto and I as part of his pack to the degree that we might also do that? Indeed, it was a very rare thing to see him uncovering those treats afterward and I relished the day, toward the end, when I stepped outside to see him burying a chicken wing under the earth to the left of the staircase outside our laundry, a hiding place I had previously been unaware of. Fortunately, I was quiet enough that he didn't notice me and I was able to just watch as he lovingly pushed earth over the mound with his nose until he was satisfied that it was adequately disguised and safe from theft.

One of Buster's favourite pastimes – jumping up to keep the seat warm for mum or dad, checking out the view from the passenger &/or driver's seat.

Chapter 21. Attention Absolute

The delight and wonder I felt observing Buster's quaint behaviours over the course of his life was likely quite similar to what a parent enjoys in watching their children learning to walk and talk and try new things. It is not only a reminder of where we all began and the process of life, but also allows us a moment or two to stop whatever we are doing or not doing and just be. Being present to the wonder and mystery of life. Taking time to just see who and what is before us or to sit and be with ourselves and hear what our soul wants us to know. Giving our undivided attention to the stirring in our heart, the words that want to be spoken, the song that wants to be sung, the hand that wants to be held and the joy that yearns to be felt. All these and more await our attention and require us to put aside all else to be privy to those messages.

I'm the elder now! ...

Stage Four
The Final Chapter

Maudsland | Gold Coast North | QLD
December 2016-December 2017

Chapter 22. Everyone Loves Buster

> *'Until one has loved an animal a part of one's soul remains unawakened.'*
>
> **Anatole France**

Not long after Buster came into our lives I suggested, tongue-in-cheek, that perhaps we could make a TV show called 'Everyone Loves Buster' given his incredible appeal to people of all ages and temperaments. There were many who commented on his gentleness – both with humans and animals – and I rarely came across a dog who didn't want to play with him. The greatest joy for me was to see the love he gave and received from the children in our community. From little girls who ordinarily were quite scared of dogs, to rambunctious boys who loved to throw the ball for him and would pop by on the way home from school to do just that.

From the very first time he saw a small child waiting for a bus in the morning, when he was just a baby himself, it was always his way to go up to them, get down to their level on the ground and cuddle up. It was a rare occasion that they did not respond with a tummy tickle and sighs of, "Isn't he cute?"

Bustie had two key fans in our early days at Bonogin, Jake and his friend, Rob, who were both great with dogs. Their joy at calling to him on their way to and from school was a delight to behold. I would smile to myself on hearing Rob call out to Jake on his way up the hill from the Bus Stop, "Jake, Buster's out!" to ensure he hurried up and didn't miss out on seeing him. Then there was the day that five boys, some of whom no doubt would have had pets of their own and some I hadn't met before, stopped at the top of our driveway, all for the express purpose of seeing Buster and throwing the ball for him. I was so lucky to hear one of them sing out, "Isn't he a cool dog?" Even now, when I recall that day, it brings tears of joy and pride to my eyes.

Many years later, in the local park in Maudsland, where a mature group of women were engaged in a morning fitness class, Buster demonstrated that he'd not lost any of his charm. Although we were on our way out of the park, Buster was obviously curious to find out what all the noise

Chapter 22. Everyone Loves Buster

was about on the other side. In his determined fashion he dragged me, pulling on his lead, across the park over to the group at the base of the staircase following the instructions of their sprightly male instructor. As we approached them, to my surprise, my neighbour Maree, saw us and called out Buster's name. Within moments, four other women had joined her to say hello and pat Buster while their instructor, now minus half his class, watched on, bemused. Where he had once attracted the attention of little boys when he was one himself, now, as an octogenarian, Buster had captured the hearts of women who could both appreciate and relate to his much older and wiser frame, something that touched my own heart on what was to be one of our last walks in that park.

Now who says, "It's a dog's life."?

Just as he was for myself and Roberto, Buster was also a welcome source of love for those who offered to look after him on the rare occasions that we went away. Despite it being our first and only chance of getting Buster to trial a pet motel while he was still young, our friends, who dearly loved him, were horrified at the thought and offered to take care of him rather than subject our precious boy to confinement in a kennel, even if it had come highly recommended. And so began many a visit to his Uncle Derek and Aunty Fran's house, where he was spoilt like a long-lost relative and after which we were lucky to have him return home with us! The vivacity with which he would race into their house as soon as his feet hit the ground, running back and forth between us, was proof of just how special their bond was. Like a child dropped off at school whose tears fade as soon as their mother or father leave, no sooner had the door closed, than Buster was comfortably settling in to his own holiday with his beloved extended family. Moving to Carrara brought us even closer to our special friends and the opportunity to bump into one another while out walking or to pop over for a cuppa. Fran and Derek were to Buster what Trusted Adults are to our children; a priceless gift to both parents and child.

photo courtesy Elena Viola

Chapter 22. Everyone Loves Buster

When I reflect on what it was that so attracted others to Buster, it was, quite simply, his presence; his unassuming, yet confident nature that made room for others to just be. And yes, I guess the way he walked and his overall appearance was endearing. Even in his later years people still called him cute or commented on what a fine looking elder gentleman he was. Another occasion to be thankful for came the day we were walking along the promenade at The Broadwater and a lovely lady asked to take a photograph of Buster for her Facebook page, 'The Dogs We Meet'. Seeing him featured there, knowing that his time was growing ever nearer, was a bitter-sweet gift that was as unexpected as it was appreciated and a reminder of his enduring appeal.

Chapter 23.
Mummy's Little Helper

'The greatest gifts you can give your children are the roots of responsibility and the wings of independence.'

Denis Waitley

I often referred to Buster as 'Mummy's Little Helper'. Apart from the fact that he just loved to be near me and other people, at different times, Buster took on a responsibility which proved helpful to both myself and my clients. The first official role he assumed happened by chance and set the precedent for his future occupation.

Whilst it was a rare occurrence for clients to ever meet Buster in our first home, when we moved to Bonogin, he enjoyed a whole new level of freedom and connectedness. My consulting room was at the back of the house and, unless it was raining, my

Chapter 23. Mummy's Little Helper

clients would ring the doorbell to let me know they had arrived, I'd call out "Come on 'round," and they would then follow the path around the side and back of the house to the studio. Invariably, by the time they arrived, Buster, having heard the chimes ring, would be there to greet them. He'd get a pat and then either sit on the step outside the room or wander off to play. Occasionally, he'd entertain us running back and forth at lightning speed across the back patio, growling happily as he shook his head from side-to-side with Cuz, his favourite toy, between his teeth. Funny as he was, they were the moments when I most empathised with parents whose toddlers do things in public that remind us how limited our power to control them is and make us want to shrink into a hole with embarrassment.

Given who he was, there was never a concern that he would break confidentiality and I don't recall anyone who found his presence a problem. On one occasion, when a young woman was crying, Buster forced open the sliding mesh door with his nose and raced in to sit by her feet and give her a cuddle. It all happened so quickly that there was no way of stopping him from expressing his protective instincts and fortunately his affections were received with a mixture of surprise and gratitude!

At other times, particularly in the heat of summer, Buster's attentions were more focused on his own need for comfort and fun. There were many occasions when he would disappear from his spot on the step and rematerialise some time later, dripping wet after high-tailing it down to the creek at the bottom of our property, for a swim to cool off. After the first heart-stopping incidence, when I knew that I could expect him to return from these sojourns, I could let go of my concern and remain focused on the task at hand. Never failing to amuse us, it acted as a lesson in the art of light-heartedness, offering a brief reprieve from what might otherwise have been a heavy session.

Then there was the day when, for some unknown reason, when the doorbell rang, instead of waiting for my client to come around, I flippantly asked Buster to go and get him. Being someone he knew well, who had always taken the time to play with him, Buster happily obliged. To see him leading the way, walking in front of my client, was such a delightful thing done with such purposefulness and from that day forward – as long as it was okay with them – Buster would always accompany my clients on the path to my room. Clearly Buster loved to be with and around people and the quaint little things he did just made him all the more endearing. Whether Buster's presence made things a little unorthodox or not – or perhaps **because** it did – my primary focus was always on my clients and their process and his antics helped

Chapter 23. Mummy's Little Helper

to dissolve a layer of seriousness which allowed us to put things into perspective again. Buster's contributions to the session were a bonus, a part of the package for those who were attracted to working with me in the way that I worked. And I would share with them the same stories I am in this book to help illustrate a point and bring us back down to earth.

Ready to escort my clients back to the front of the house after their session.

In our home in Carrara, where for his safety, Buster had to be locked into the backyard, greeting clients was more a hit-and-miss phenomenon and generally took the form of a quick hello before he was hurried back through the side gate. Although there was the odd occasion when, either because he stubbornly refused to go, or on the request of the client, he would remain in the studio for the duration of the session. Whilst this became the home in which we lived together for the longest, the majority of the time he spent with me was when I moved my office out of the studio and back upstairs to work from inside the house, specifically so that he could be near me and free to come and go as he chose.

As happens when we are too busy living life to notice the subtleties, once again the move to his last home in Maudsland brought home to us what had been missing for Buster in those years at Carrara, something for which I will be forever grateful. Here in this quiet little street only 3.5 km from the highway, home felt like being in the country once more. Abundant bird life, snakes, turtles, water dragons and ducks in the nearby creek and a tawny frog mouth, a deeply mystical, owl-like creature who would perch on our Hills Hoist clothes line while Buster sat beneath it on moonlit nights, made for a stimulating natural environment for him and us to enjoy. Of course, there were the dreaded cane-toads whose appearance was tempered by the delightful geckos who had also been a consistent part of our lives in this part of the world. It took a while when we first moved up from Sydney to discover that the noises we were hearing were coming from these tiny creatures. There was many a time we would

Chapter 23. Mummy's Little Helper

beg their forgiveness for inadvertently cutting off a tail or leg when they got lodged between, or had been sleeping inside, the cavity of the sliding doors and windows. A search of Wikipedia reveals a host of superstitions to explain their behaviours and the sounds they make, but essentially, they are considered quite unique as one of the few species who actually have a voice: a symbol which proved useful in working with my clients.

What also delighted us about this home on Buster's behalf, was that once more he was free to roam within the boundaries of our block and could be found at any given time, depending on his mood, either attached to the back fence having a chin-wag with the dog who lived on the other side, hanging out on the front balcony watching life go by or at the front fence ready to greet passers-by and those whose business belonged to our home. He had numerous hidey-holes to keep him cool and covered areas to either escape the heat or keep out of the elements when they were less-than inviting.

But of all these, none was a greater reminder of what had potentially been missing in Carrara, or more satisfying to me, than his re-connection from both outside and within the house, to my consulting room. As was our routine, if I had been working upstairs prior to their arrival, whenever I had a client, I would put Buster outside with a treat, recite what had become a lengthy farewell spiel and then head downstairs to begin work. Once again, what had always been the trigger to alert Buster to the arrival of my clients, the sound of the doorbell chiming, would bring him running to the top of the outside stairs to check things out. Once he knew that folk were here, he'd come on down and sit on the pavers in the covered area adjacent to my room. Sometimes we would be unaware of his presence, perhaps just hearing his soft breathing as he slept outside the sliding door. At other, times, he'd announce himself with a clipped bark and at a convenient time, we'd bring him into the room to be with us. As soon as I opened the door, he'd run in, go straight to my clients, push himself up against their legs for a cuddle and stay until he could feel that he'd done his job. Then he'd walk a few steps away, let out a sigh and plonk himself down on the rug with his back to us, content to just be without any further interruption until the session was over, when he would escort them to the front door to say goodbye.

As he grew older and his hearing began to fail him, he may have missed that initial indication that it was time to get to work and it would only be after some time when he'd either finished devouring his treat or sensed that I was actually still home, that he would make his way down the stairs once more. What never ceased to amaze

Chapter 23. Mummy's Little Helper

me was how seriously he took his job. Most of the time when I was with clients, no one else was at home. However, in the early evenings, when Roberto was home and he had his dad to hang out with, he would still come down to join us, which totally blew me away. The indication that Buster was on his way was the sound of his paws descending the timber staircase, followed by a more muffled noise as he made his way across the tiles to sit with his nose peering under the doorway, patiently waiting to be noticed. Of course, I would always wait until an appropriate break to ask permission before getting up to let him in, which no doubt would ease my clients' feeling of being watched.

The one time when he didn't do that because he could no longer safely go down the stairs alone, I had a new client whose friend had referred her to me and actually told her about Buster. Not wanting to disappoint her and mindful that this might be her only opportunity to meet him, at the end of our session I took her upstairs before she left so that they could say hello to one another. Even though he continues to be a part of my practice through the stories I tell of him and his eternal presence in Spirit, in writing this now I know that it's just not the same without him and that, sadly, – as for all of us in relation to those we have loved and lost – it is just how it is!

I often wonder if, as he sat in the room with us, he took on some of the energy that was connected to my clients and their lives or provided some kind of gateway through which a new, simpler possibility could be found. There were many moments of synchronicity that suggested that he may actually have been taking in more than we had imagined. There is one that sticks most in my mind which was both illuminating and very funny and perhaps a farewell gift from Buster to my client and her family. As often occurs, it is only after exhausting every other option, of doing everything we know to do, that we may fall to our knees and be willing to try or even entertain that there is something else we could do, or not do, as may be the case. I honour the people whose commitment to their own growth and healing and desire for an easier life experience has them persist until that crack opens through which the light can shine.

With such a transformation imminent and after grappling with what that meant for her, we were both jolted out of the conversation when in reply to her pleading, "Do you mean all I have to do is …?" from outside the room on the pavers came a sound I only ever heard Buster make that one time. Whatever meaning we gave to it, it acted as validation for her question and brought us both unstuck with laughter. It was as if he was saying "Hallelujah! It's about time!" or "Yes, by Jove, I

Chapter 23. Mummy's Little Helper

think you've got it!" At which point, his job, for that day at least, was done!

Just as it did for Buster, there is a pride and sense of purpose that develops in children when given responsibility. We all want to know that we matter, that there is something we can contribute and that we can be trusted to get the job done, even if a little clumsily at first. Allowing children to take on tasks at home and school, to learn how to do the basic 'stuff' of life, rather than having everything done for them, helps to build the competence that leads to confidence, essential elements of a budding self-respect. By developing an understanding of life's ups and downs and giving them something bigger than themselves to focus on, children become more resilient and less susceptible to the grip of anxiety or depression. With responsibility to and for oneself, come many life-skills, the possibility of much more enriching relationships with others and success in life itself.

Chapter 24.
The Things We Do for Love

> *'A mother's love for her child is like nothing else in the world. It knows no law, no pity, it dares all things and crushes down remorselessly all that stands in its path.'*
>
> **Agatha Christie**

As parents, we do things for our children that the majority of people would do for no one else. Watching my husband pick up our friend's newborn baby boy in the half-light of his home-birth sanctuary to change his nappy in the first years of our marriage, absolutely blew me away and to this day, I am still a little cautious when faced with that task in one so small. Roberto had no compunction about changing a pooey nappy in a tiny baby who wasn't even his own and he did it with great aplomb.

Chapter 24. The Things We Do for Love

Many years later, it surprised me that I would stop to observe Buster as he went about his morning ablutions to ensure that his body was functioning properly and that when we were out, I would collect them to help keep our neighbourhood clean. The first time I took out a plastic bag to collect Buster's poos on our morning walk was a defining moment in our relationship. Seriously! I remember the way he looked at me and how he related to me thereafter; it was as if to say, "If you'd do that for me, then you must be my Mummy!" Of course, this is completely my interpretation and I can still see the expression on his face that day. It was a bonding moment, the action that said I was prepared to do whatever it took to be his mum, even collecting something that had been a part of him and come from inside his body.

However, this paled into insignificance in comparison with the multitude of times I put my hand right into Buster's mouth to administer supplements or medication. A task I would never have believed I was capable of, let alone how confidently and determinedly I did it in the face of a very stubborn canine, who was as committed to spitting them out from the corners of his mouth, as I was of ensuring that they found their way into his tummy. Despite Buster's attempts at defying me, there was only ever one time, when we were both scared and tired toward the end, that I risked being bitten by him when my hand was inside his well-toothed mouth. When I recall the bones he was able to obliterate in a mere matter of moments, it was amazing that he never used those teeth to hurt me, or anyone else, in his lifetime and that I trusted that I was safe to do this.

Somewhere in my consciousness I knew a time would come when love would also guide me to lie with him; to take my place on the ground – albeit on a mattress – so that I could be with him, talk to and comfort him to see him through his final days here on Earth. When I found myself doing that, it came from both a knowing that the time had come and the devastation that he and I and

Chapter 24. The Things We Do for Love

Roberto had reached this point. In the same way, when we made the decision to release him from his physical body, as excruciating as it was, it was done with love absolute.

I think that, like self-discipline, it is the willingness to do the things we really don't want to do but know are the right things to do, that allows us to surprise ourselves and others when we are called upon to step outside our comfort zones. There are so many things we do for love and rarely do we consider them a burden or sacrifice. In this way, as we give to others, we grow and become more of the men and women we were meant to be. The sheer satisfaction of getting my job done as a mother to Buster, seeing this little creature be so happy and healthy, made every action worth whatever it took. This is the privilege of being a parent and when we stretch ourselves to fill those shoes we are left with a sense of wholeness that nothing and no one can take away from us.

Chapter 25. Warning Signs

'Pay attention to the little things. They're more important than you think.'

Matt Gutierrez

As I woke on the morning that marked the first calendar month since Buster's passing, in our newly-curtained bedroom – darker, cooler and quieter than it had been up until now – I reflected on what we had noticed in the months preceding that in some ways had confused and saddened us. At no time to my knowledge did we make the connection that what was happening foretold the future that was to unfold. For the first time, it was apparent to me that Buster was not only withdrawing from us for his own sake, but also giving us the opportunity to begin to experience what it would be like to be without him. I recall many a

Chapter 25. Warning Signs

conversation between Roberto and I making light of Buster's changed behaviour; suggesting that he was being like a teenager not wanting to hang out with Mummy and Daddy anymore 'cause it wasn't cool. For someone who had sought to be with us at all times wherever we were, this was something we were not only unaccustomed to, but unable to recognise for what it was.

Buster was beginning to let go, to seek quiet in his own space and perhaps to begin to be used to being without us as much as putting us in a position to be without him. No doubt, he was also reserving his energy for when he wanted to make contact and engage. In her own way, I noticed my mother had done the same prior to her transition; keeping to herself, not being there as much as she had in the past, giving less room for my conversation and wanting only to talk about what she needed to in the brief time she had that was comfortable for her to talk on the phone. Thankfully, at those times, I would be quiet and just listen so she could speak and be heard uninterrupted, something which now gives me a measure of peace.

These warning signs that our loved ones give us often go unnoticed or noticed and misunderstood and therefore not responded to in right manner. While literature about behaviour changes to expect in old dogs refers to changes such as those we observed in Buster, in human beings, the same withdrawal may be indicative of an equally serious issue. Whether it be heralding the end of a relationship or marriage or a sign that someone has come to the end of their tether and is contemplating taking their own life, being willing to ask the question, "Are you okay?" or "How can I help?" may just open the door to a far different outcome. What was once considered dangerous and possibly suggestive; to ask someone directly "Are you thinking of suicide or hurting yourself?" actually makes room for them to acknowledge their thoughts and feelings and begin to talk about what is really going on for them[3].

Quiet Time for Buster

Chapter 25. Warning Signs

In the same way, many partners give up after their attempts to communicate their despair about their relationship has either been poorly conveyed, misinterpreted or fallen on deaf ears. Frequently at the heart of relationship breakdown is a feeling of unfulfilled expectations, the disappointment of needs not being met. How often do we see or sense that something isn't as it should be or as it was and not know what to do about it, or be so acculturated to it that it ceases to be a cause for concern or attention and just becomes the 'new normal'? No doubt this is what happens when relationships break down, particularly when one of the partners says they didn't see it coming, despite the fact that the warning signs were staring them in the face, often for years on end.

There are many situations where, for whatever reason, we feel incapable of communicating what we're feeling or what we need. Children in particular can be hamstrung either by their lack of vocabulary to describe the pain they are in or because, in instances of bullying or child abuse in particular, they have been sworn to secrecy. Take notice of the subtle changes in behaviour and temperament and look deeper to find the source of what is often dismissed as just a phase they are going through. Children and young people depend on us to be able to read between the lines and will often tell us what they think we want to hear, rather than what's really going on for them.

Perhaps the signs we least want to acknowledge are those which indicate that our physical wellbeing is compromised. Pain and discomfort are the body's way of telling us that all is not well or that there are changes we need to make in our lives. If we ignore the symptoms in the early stages and don't take responsibility for our wellbeing, things can potentially worsen and develop into illness and disease. By paying attention and recognising the warning signs we will be in a much better position to seek the help we need and minimise the harm that might otherwise eventuate.

Sometimes, it is only on reflection that we are able to see things for what they are. In our case, I suspect we may have misread the changes in Buster's behaviour, who obviously couldn't tell us in words, when he stopped hanging out in the kitchen with Roberto in the morning as he had always done. What we attributed to hearing loss or ageing taste buds, when he would spit out the last piece of toast that he had once eagerly waited for each day, may instead have been a sign that something else was going on. Even so, I am sure there are times, particularly when our capacity to effect a change in a situation is limited, that we

Chapter 25. Warning Signs

are spared knowing everything; that we are not meant to tempt fate and instead must accept that life is a mystery.

---

(3) **Always** seek professional help in such situations and be aware of your own limitations. These are not times to keep secrets! Call your local Suicide Prevention Hotline or the Emergency Department of your nearest hospital who can direct you to the assistance available.

Chapter 26.
The Importance of Trusting Yourself

> *'Learning to trust yourself and what you know takes time and work. You cannot expect to eradicate a lifetime of misguided information overnight. You must make a continuous, conscious effort to get on good terms with you.'*
>
> **Iyanla Vanzant**

When I think of the words 'trust yourself', it seems they are synonymous with two other things: self-respect and self-belief. All three require that we pay attention to ourselves; to the still, quiet voice within that is always connected to our truth and seeks only to be at peace with and honour our highest knowing or intuition. Trusting ourselves is something we do automatically from birth

Chapter 26. The Importance of Trusting Yourself

and yet it is also the very thing that begins to be whittled away the moment our truth is either questioned by another or our survival demands that we agree with their truth over our own. As our greatest needs are for love and belonging, and we are born into a family system which has its own conscience and set of unspoken rules that govern its membership, we do what it is that will assure our place in the tribe. Similarly, dogs come with the intrinsic knowledge of what it takes to belong to the pack. And yet, despite this, Buster consistently demonstrated to me his ability to honour his truth in each moment.

I recall the words of Lorna Patten, one of my first teachers, who told me that the most important thing I needed to learn in order to do my work was how to trust myself. Obviously, there was and continues to be much more learning and training that informs my practice and yet, without that trust in myself and a willingness to be vigilant in both my motives and my actions, all the knowledge in the world would be of limited use. It takes courage to be true to ourselves and to trust that truth when someone or something outside ourselves might challenge it, whether it is assumed or actual. And so, when I pass on that same advice to my clients, and in particular to parents, I am patently aware that it is much easier said than done.

Just as there is a pull to toe the party line in a family, the same is true among couples. Being able to achieve a degree of intimacy while also retaining your autonomy or sovereignty as an individual in relationship with another, is often a very challenging juggling act. The cost of not speaking up and threatening that harmony can however, also be something that has life-long implications. The challenge, when you know that something is the right action to take, in the face of disagreement or a momentary difference of opinion with another; especially one whom you love and trust, is to tell your whole truth. Whilst no doubt there were many such instances over the course of Buster's life there are two which really stand out that I will always reflect on with gratitude and peace.

The first was a decision Roberto and I made together after making the connection that, for the second year in a row following his annual vaccination, Buster was seriously ill, causing us both great concern and substantial cost in Veterinarian fees. In this instance, it was not a matter of our disagreeing with one another, but rather having to confront the Vet with what we believed was the actual cause of Buster's malaise. When something that was intended to protect him had actually threatened his wellbeing to such an extent, we had to question not only the

Chapter 26. The Importance of Trusting Yourself

necessity, but also the validity of continuing to do this again in the future. It was something we did as his parents and with great conviction, which no doubt prepared us for the difficult decisions we would have to make many years down the track when trusting ourselves and being aligned in our choices on Buster's behalf would tolerate no compromise.

At the time, the Vet accepted our proposal and after the blood tests showed both the cause of his illness and the evidence that his body had already accumulated sufficient amounts of vaccine after a number of annual injections, he compensated us by reducing the fees and recommending that Buster no longer needed to have the booster shots. To my knowledge, this was and still is not, information that is common or even recommended protocol, however, from that time on, Buster never had another of those vaccinations, something that gave Roberto and myself much peace of mind. If I had known then that there were also other, more natural alternatives to the monthly medication that he did have, I would most definitely have looked into that in greater depth too!

The second was as difficult as it was imperative, as it not only related to Buster's wellbeing, but also represented me honouring what I knew to be my truth in the face of a different opinion from

Roberto, when all three of us were feeling our most vulnerable. I'm sure anyone who has been in a long-term relationship will understand me when I say that there are times that I look back upon and wish I had stood by my own conviction rather than allowing myself to be swayed in my husband's direction. Always it seems that in the darkest moments we are called upon to take risks, to step out of our comfort zones and do what we know we must or live forever more regretting that we hadn't. While on the surface it was a relatively simple thing, making that choice was a truly liberating experience and one which I know will serve as the reminder of what is possible for me, and others, moving forward.

On what turned out to be Buster's last swim ten days out from his passing, he and I had spent much of the day at home inside. There was a moment when I looked at him and my heart felt as if someone had stuck a fish hook into it and wrenched it out of my chest. For the first time he looked really, really old, tired beyond his years and when he looked at me it felt as if he was saying his time was drawing ever nearer. Even now as I write this, five months down the track, I know if I connect too closely with how I felt at the time, it would be almost impossible to breathe. When Roberto came home that afternoon on what had been a rather hot December day I suggested that

Chapter 26. The Importance of Trusting Yourself

we take Buster for a swim and get us all out of the house and down to The Broadwater, which was our closest waterway. At about this time, Roberto was aware of the desperation I had been displaying, wanting to be with Buster as much as I could; sometimes, as he said, not giving our boy space, following him around to see that he was okay and at times crumbling into a blubber of tears whenever I saw him struggling to stand or walk. So, when Buster left the room we'd been in and walked out to lie on his stretcher on the deck, Roberto's inclination was for me to let him be. At the time, I might easily have not taken this any further.

Whatever it was that had me go back to Buster and ask again if he wanted to go for a swim, words we knew he understood from a lifetime of use, I will be eternally grateful for. In that moment, I absolutely trusted myself, trusted that even though Buster was tired, even though Roberto had said no, that it was the right thing to do. Somehow the mother in me knew that this was what was needed and was worth standing my ground for. So, rather than ask, I told Roberto and Buster that we were going for a swim, to which he responded by getting up from his bed and we gathered his swimmers – the life-jacket he had worn for the past few years to lessen the impact on his hips – and our towels and off we went.

Although it was brief, the joy tinged with sadness that I felt at once more being able to swim with Bustie, watching his little legs paddling away under the water on that beautiful Sunday afternoon, was absolutely priceless. And when, as he had always done, I left him to sit with Roberto on the sand to have a dip on my own, he ran back down to the water's edge to 'rescue' me, we laughed tears of joy. This was the Buster we had always known, these were moments that nothing could ever replace and no money could ever buy. As he sat facing the water, watching the boats and jet-skis whizzing by, looking so at peace, the gift was a precious one for us all. When we arrived home, he ate all his dinner for the first time in a while, no doubt with an appetite spurred on by this welcome activity and we rejoiced in seeing once more his former happy self.

Although we can never know the answer to the 'What if's?', I do know that it was my trust in myself and my insistence that I and we honour that, which rewarded us all with our experience that day and memories that I believe we will treasure forever.

Chapter 27. Time to Say Goodbye

> 'This existence of ours is as transient as autumn clouds. To watch the birth and death of beings is like looking at the movements of a dance. A lifetime is like a flash of lightning in the sky rushing by like a torrent down a steep mountain. We have stopped for a moment to encounter each other; to meet, to love, to share. This is a precious moment, but it is transient. It is a little parenthesis in eternity. If we share with caring, lightheartedness and love we will create abundance and joy for each other and then this moment will have been worthwhile.'
>
> **Gautama Buddha**

Journal Entry | Thursday, 4 January, 2018

While I'm certain I will never forget the day we said goodbye to Buster, right now it feels urgent that I take the time to write about it, already eight days ago. I am sure that no one who has ever had to make the same decision for a loved one, be it human or animal, as Roberto and myself, has ever done that without an enormous amount of soul-searching and heartache. When I lay down on the mattress beside Buster's bed on what was to be his last night, stroking his beautiful fur and giving him whatever comfort and healing I could, what I could smell on his breath, combined with the other symptoms he was displaying, told me that things were not going well. If, up until then, I had been unwilling to accept that there was something sinister taking place in his body, I could no longer deny it and I knew that its hold on him was far greater than any relief I or anyone else could offer him.

Although it had originally been my intention to lie with him all night – which I now know was more for me than something that he needed – after a while, I 'heard' him tell me to go and let him be. No sooner had I stood up, than he turned around in his bed to face the wall and went to sleep. That night he slept so soundly, with no coughing or even snoring that I wonder sometimes whether he knew

Chapter 27. Time to Say Goodbye

that we were all preparing to let him go. On those nights lying down with him on the floor, cradling his little head, with my hand beneath his chin, his paws entwined around my arm, I experienced the all-encompassing sweetness that defined this creature of God's.

It is so hard to put into words the things we experienced that day. Each moment and every incident that took place was perfect and irreplaceable and will serve to bring us peace – along with buckets of tears – whenever we recall them. When I woke in the morning just before dawn, I saw that a number of the objects on my bedside table had mysteriously moved and were facing in Buster's direction. This was my first note to self. The image of Buster lying with his chin resting on the mattress in front of his bed with my life-sized Pooh bear on the floor beside him, was one of absolute peace. All around the room it seemed that objects were watching over him and none of this escaped my attention.

As we sat eating breakfast on the front balcony, Buster's favourite morning hang-out, my oldest and dearest friend, Julie, on holidays in England, knowing how urgent was my need to talk to her, finally managed to connect with me on Messenger. As she had always done, Julie shared with me her wisdom, reassuring me that we would know what the right thing to do would be. That she, like Elena, my sister-in-law, both of whom absolutely loved Buster, was able to say goodbye to him over the net is something for which I will always be indebted to technology for. Knowing that we would most likely be faced with some tough decisions when we saw the Vet that morning, I made sure that Roberto and I discussed the pending visit, but never with the thought that today would be the day.

With an appointment in place for mid-morning, I suggested we go to what had been the location of our Sunday afternoon family outings for half of Buster's life by the little beach at Emerald Lakes, for a last visit there together. When we arrived, there was a group of elderly people sailing remote-controlled model yachts on the water, something we'd not encountered before, and as Buster walked toward them, it seemed there was a knowing we shared which went beyond the spoken word. Looking back now, I smile when I think of the irony of it; that here was the miniature version of the yachts we might otherwise have lived among, with the family we built in its stead. At this time, Buster walked briskly compared to what we had become used to and in the cool morning breeze, we took photos and selfies which captured the moments beautifully. This act of saying goodbye was also something Bustie had

Chapter 27. Time to Say Goodbye

been doing himself in the weeks prior, spending invaluable time in all his favourite places in and out of the house and I was so pleased to see him do that, especially when I caught him hiding one of his frozen chicken necks in his hidey hole outside our back door.

In his own way, Buster taught us a lot about respect and how to appreciate the quirky behaviours that are unique to each of us, without ever needing or wanting to change him or them. It was always as if we were observing a baby or youngster learning how to walk or exploring their environment for the first time. He never lost that puppy-sense that was so delightful to witness. And nothing was ever too much for us to do for him. Yes, we laughed many a time about what a great life he had and how we would want to come back as a dog in a home like ours. That, I guess, is something to be proud of. Dogs and children are our most gentle and sensitive beings and they deserve all the love, protection, nurturing and joy we can offer.

Nothing prepared us for the moment when the Vet explained what was actually happening in Buster's body, or the prognosis of what would unfold over a period of just three weeks if we did not make the choice to euthanise him. Observing Buster sitting on the floor and listening to us recount recent events, her experience told her that the time had come to relieve his pain and to confront us with the reality that there would be no more sleeps for Buster; that the only humane choice we had was whether to do it then and there or later in the day. Clearly in shock, eased only by her physical inspection of Buster and replies to my urgent questions, having blindly thought that there may still have been something we could do, we chose the latest possible appointment that day and set out to make the most of the time left to us together as a family.

Nature, unsurprisingly, was one of Buster's great loves and, just as we had done earlier that day, we headed out to another of our favourite places, the beach where we had spent the most time together over the years. After eating lunch in a café, with Bustie sitting beneath us, his head resting on the legs of the table, we went across the road to Miami Beach. Looking back now I am amazed that either of us was able to stomach anything that day and yet this too was one of the things we loved to share with our boy; being out doing coffee or lunch. Helping him walk on the sand and lay down to face the ocean as he had done countless times before, I was overcome with emotion and the realisation of both the task which lay ahead of us and how ready he was for it. He was 'dog tired' and made no attempt to either sit up or to

Chapter 27. Time to Say Goodbye

walk around and explore as he would normally have done. Looking at the sky, it was as if a space had opened up in the clouds just for him, letting us know that Heaven and our loved ones were preparing for his arrival and that all would be well. While I'll never know for sure, I hope that the time he spent lying on the sand, feeling its warmth on his tummy and in his paws, was something that felt good to him and recalled fond memories of a lifetime of experiences he loved.

From here, Roberto took us on a beautiful drive through the Hinterland and up into Beechmont, a gentle jaunt that gave us more time together to reflect and share. While time did not permit us to visit other friends or family, we were grateful to have been able to coordinate our return home with the opportunity to say goodbye to our friend, Jules and her children, who had recently built a relationship with Buster. They had cared for him during our time in Sydney after my mother's passing and we were aware that his sudden absence would be difficult and confusing for them if they had not made that connection.

Although I had wanted to take Buster back through our home one last time when we stopped there, I now appreciate Roberto's wisdom in refusing to do that, knowing that it would have been even more excruciating to leave again to do what we had to do. As Roberto went inside to collect what we needed, I lifted Buster out of the car and placed his four paws on the ground to take in the energy from the earth that had supported and held him in his last home. As I did, a brief sun shower filled the sky and touched us ever so lightly as if to offer purification before this final journey. As we drove up the hill toward the highway, a rainbow filled the sky, another sign that Heaven was preparing to receive him and with tears welling up, I hastily captured a photo on my iPhone from inside the car, an omen that was both gracious and timely.

Despite traveling with Buster in our vehicles for the whole of his life without ever tying him down, we had only recently purchased his first harness and seat cover to use in Roberto's new car. This gave him the opportunity to lie down comfortably and safely in the back seat and me the chance to sit beside him and hold him on that last voyage. As we drove along, he took his final drink of water from my hand in small amounts, one more blessing and unforgettable kinaesthetic memory for me. Despite his age, his tongue was still as soft as it was when he was a baby and it felt like the ultimate gift to be able to help him drink in that way at that time.

As I write this, I think about how intricate the details of that last day are and wonder if a reader

Chapter 27. Time to Say Goodbye

would consider it indulgent. Then I think about how we might reflect on the last day of anyone we love and the way it either nourishes or haunts us. I am humbled by that day and its memories and know that it will be an ongoing source of comfort, as we move forward without Buster's physical presence in our lives or this home, but forever in our hearts and minds.

The way Buster walked back into the Vet's Surgery that afternoon, after stopping to relieve himself and take in the scents in the garden outside, indicated that he knew what was about to unfold and he was in agreement with it. He was so dignified, a beautiful creature with eyes still bright, a still-shiny coat, despite all else. When we entered the reception area nearing the close of business, there was just one other family present discussing their dog's treatment. As I stood with Buster near the doorway, Roberto went over to check in with the receptionist. As soon as the father realised our purpose in being there, he expressed his condolences to Roberto, and, close to tears, came straight over to see Buster and I. As I have experienced so many times since living on the Gold Coast, albeit for quite different reasons, this family showed a degree of empathy and compassion that will stay with me 'til the end of my days.

They had two beautiful little boys, one dressed in shorts, vest and tie, looking very dapper indeed, something his mother said he loved to wear as often as he could. As they sat on the floor with Buster, patting and talking to him, I was taken back to those balmy summer mornings at the Bus Stop in Banora Point where he first encountered little ones and it seemed his life had come full-circle. An unmistakable act of reciprocity, coming from people we had just met, giving back to him the love he had given so fully and respecting him now as an elder, seemed like the perfect farewell for this gentle creature who had given and received so much love throughout his lifetime and been such a gift to so many children, young and old. When they left, the parents, only minutes before, complete strangers, hugged us and offered their sympathies, themselves having been through what we were about to, leaving us ever grateful for such an unexpected and welcome act of kindness.

For now, the telling of this story has felt considerably more painful than the experience itself, no doubt because on the day, to some degree, I was in survival mode, doing what was necessary to get through it, before having to face the reality of his passing. Suffice to say, the hardest part was yet to come and so I will keep it brief for you and for myself. It is important to

Chapter 27. Time to Say Goodbye

mention however, that there is much to be said for voluntary euthanasia, in light of what is a far more humane act we offer our animal friends. Applied to all sentient beings, not only would it give us the opportunity to ease their suffering and end their lives with dignity, but also to cease the administration of costly, unnecessary and sometimes ineffective, treatments.

Having explained the process to us earlier that day, the Vet reminded us once more what would happen and, true to her word, Buster's passing was swift and free of drama. With Roberto at his side and me maintaining eye contact with him, as I had promised I would do, he slipped into a peaceful sleep in a matter of moments. For both Roberto and myself this was such a merciful act and a privilege to witness. There were no body twitches to startle us and nothing released from his body. As always, our boy retained his composure, a gentleman to the end. Perhaps as a final gesture of thanks to the woman who performed this unenviable task, just before he closed his eyes, his right eye moved ever so slowly to look in her direction and then returned once more to centre before the lid closed for the last time.

I think the most beautiful thing Buster did for us was to time his ending with when Roberto and I could both be there with him. For the last six weeks of his life, one or both of us was here all the time, apart from two occasions when we went to do the shopping and on Christmas Day. I know that I was tempted before and after not to leave him that day and yet it was also important to be with family too. Sitting here now I realise that – just as I had felt with my mother – I had been living with an underlying anxiety that something might happen to him when we were not around and that we would come home to find him either hurt as a result of over-extending himself or worse still, having passed over in our absence. And there was just no way that I would ever have wanted him to be without us at that time.

When I think of Buster lying on that bed in the Vet's room so peaceful, and as beautiful and whole as he had ever been, with Roberto and I beside him, I could think of no better way to have let him go, or for him to have been relieved of his suffering, as much as his absence now causes us immeasurable pain and sorrow. I think this was the most selfless act we have ever performed. To ease the pain of one you love so much, even when it involves denying yourself their physical presence, is the ultimate act of love. I guess the equivalent of that in human life is to do or say whatever it is that a loved one is wanting to hear or see that will allow them to let go, when they too are ready and their time has come. I had always wanted to

Chapter 27. Time to Say Goodbye

be there with my mother at the end and to do the things I did with and for Buster. While that wasn't to be my destiny, I got to experience that as a mother and to see the absolute peace that comes at the moment of death and a life well-lived. Mum said many a time that she wanted that for me and I know in my heart that she helped make that possible for both Roberto and I with our beloved boy. I am also so glad for all of us that I encouraged Roberto to be there when Bustie was euthanised and that, just as we had done when we first found him, we did it together.

Chapter 28.
The Gift of Life

'I expect to pass through this world but once. Any good, therefore, that I can do or any kindness I can show to any fellow creature, let me do it now. Let me not defer or neglect it for I shall not pass this way again.'

Stephen Grellet

Journal Entry | Sunday, 25 March, 2018

Oddly enough it wasn't until Buster had been gone for almost three months that I realised something that was of vital importance to me. Namely, that although I had been working with parents in one way or another for more than 25 years, it was only since being a mother to Bustie that I felt I had some authority to address the issue of parenting with a wider audience and under my own steam.

Chapter 28. The Gift of Life

While there are many differences between parenting a child and a dog, the one thing that remains fundamental to both is that it be done with love unconditional. And that came effortlessly with Buster! In truth, I also always knew that the very thing that allowed me to be a good mum was my training and experience as a teacher in Primary and Special Education and having grown up in an extended family where children were cherished. To this day, there are children whose stories I tell to share the lessons they taught me and for whom I will always be thankful. What I learnt to apply with children became the strategies I used to raise Buster and I have to say I was always proud of who he was, how he behaved and the acknowledgement of that in strangers and friends alike.

Going the distance with him when he was a little tacker made life so much easier as he grew and there was rarely a time that I feared for his safety, or that of other dogs, or people in his presence. When he passed, his body was whole, apart from the removal of those two, small, puppy-producing sacs that were snipped not long after first making their appearance. He suffered no broken bones, survived a tick bite, and the removal of a growth on his front right paw, playful encounters with cane toads and snakes, as well as the odd tummy problems from ingesting too much salt water. We said from the very beginning that he would never make anyone pregnant, get involved in crime or be addicted to drugs or alcohol. Buster's only addictions were to fun and connection … and food of course, though he only ever ate as much as he needed to satisfy himself at any time.

There was one ailment that Buster endured throughout his life which we discovered when he was just 7 months old. This was the reason why we had him de-sexed so as not to pass it on to future generations. Apparently rare for a staffy x kelpie breed, finding out that he was most likely born with hip dysplasia was the first time we grieved for our boy and what his future would hold. It was that diagnosis and an even more alarming prognosis delivered by the Vet, that spurred us on to do all we could to give him the happiest and healthiest life possible for as long as possible. Apart from the Vet's words on that day, I still recall the comment made by the receptionist, who said that Buster was really lucky to have us as parents, indicating that many people would let go of a puppy once they knew he had this condition because of the extra expense and uncertainty it entailed, no pun intended. In our case, while there was shock and grief associated with receiving this news, it also strengthened our commitment to rise above the label and its implications.

Chapter 28. The Gift of Life

Whilst a little of the innocence was taken from us on that day, it also meant we could adjust our routines and impose boundaries from that time forward to minimise the harm to Buster and his body. While he loved to play with other dogs in the park and on the beach, we would make sure they didn't jump on his back in their playful exchanges. In the same way, while we want our children to have fun, putting boundaries and limits in place from the very beginning helps them to learn more about their own boundaries and what it takes to be safe. Over time, we adjusted the way he played at home too so that there was less chance for him to hurt his hips and spine when running and jumping. If left to him, Buster would have kept playing until his own pain stopped him; it was therefore our job to impose the limits that short-circuited that so that he would be well enough to play another day.

As Buster grew older and my life became busier, I realised that the occasions on which we played together had seriously declined and our daily walks were stretching out into intervals that served neither one of us. Thankfully, he rarely let his dad go off to work in the morning without playing fetch, which was part of their morning routine, before Roberto said his goodbyes for the day. It was then that Buster and I would head out for a walk or swim depending on where we were living at the time. What never, ever ceased to enchant me was the sheer delight

Buster expressed, particularly if it had been a few days since our last walk, and the reminder of the joy inherent in life's simplest pleasures. Despite all the gadgets we have and all the fast-paced entertainment available to children, I still believe that it is the simplest of things – a bucket of pegs for instance in the tiniest ones – that intrigue and make use of their natural inquisitiveness and creativity. When we, as parents, make the time to sit and play or read and draw with our children, or engage in any form of outside play or sport, we are not only modelling this for them, but building a connection and memory bank from which they will draw and be nourished by into the future.

As a mother, I was most content when I knew that all was well with Buster. Even if it meant that I missed out on doing something for myself, when I gave to Buster what I believed he needed, I felt happiest and most at ease. Of course, there were many times when I couldn't fulfil that edict, but the prevailing experience he enjoyed of being more than adequately cared for, compensated for those occasions. We often laughed about how smart Buster was, waiting at the shelter until we came along – suckers for his charms – ready to put aside our own needs to see to it that he was happy. And as I sit here writing this now, there is not one thing Roberto or I would change about that! In my experience, it has always been the love that I didn't

Chapter 28. The Gift of Life

feel I was free to give or was rejected by others that has hurt far more than any act of love given on my part. It is the parents who give and the children who receive. That is how the 'Orders of Love', as defined by Bert Hellinger[4], work and that is what brings peace and harmony into family life. When a parent is neither willing nor able to give, or a child is unwilling or unable to receive – life, love, sustenance, direction, among other things – from their parents or guardians, then things are out of balance and the flow of love is blocked.

Here I think we need to dispel the myth that love is a scarce commodity, though many people behave as if it is, no doubt from a belief or life experience that has taught them that. Rather, love is indefinable, has no boundaries, and when it is fully expressed, comes from a heart that is full and constantly replenished through the giving of that love in a circle from themselves out to others and back again. Sometimes how we learn to love ourselves is by loving others and seeking to answer the question "How may I serve?" rather than "What's in it for me?" So, don't wait 'til you've learnt how to do that before entering into your next relationship, because it is in the context of relationship that we learn how to love and how to let love in, not sitting on the sidelines trying to work it out. By all means, give yourself the time you need to reflect and grieve a previous relationship before embarking on a new one, but don't wait too long!

This thing called life demands that we be so much bigger than that voice in our heads; the critical or fearful one at least. It is way too short and there is so much to learn, so much to give and receive, before that last spark goes out. Of course, you can continue to learn, and if you're human, you will undoubtedly also continue to make mistakes from which to learn more, so stop expecting that it's going to be any different to that. I know that had we not made the decision to let Buster go when we did, he would have held on until his body completely gave out – a horrible ending for such an exquisite being – because not only did he have a zest for life, but, loyal to the end, he also never wanted to disappoint his mum and dad.

We need to live life with the reverence it holds for us. It is the greatest gift we will ever be granted and in most, though not all, cases, we were created in love. It is what we are made of, what we are here for and what must guide us if we are to make our way in the world and bring forth a new world order that has called to and awaited our attention and devotion since the beginnings of time. From the moment he came into my life, throughout my 'Travels with Buster', I received inestimable gifts of unconditional love that will continue to nourish my

Chapter 28. The Gift of Life

soul and inform who I am for the rest of my days. I invite you to join me in celebrating this gift of life, to experience joy and to open your heart to yourself and all sentient beings as you too travel the path of love's unconditional journey.

---

(4) The 'Orders of Love' is the term Bert Hellinger, the 'Father of Family Constellations' gives to the unconscious orders which help to keep love flowing. When everyone in a family system is included and given their rightful place, as well as being able to accept their own 'fate', then love can flow freely among the members of the family. Please see my video on 'The Orders of Love' and the Family Constellations section of my website for more information. www.positiverelating.com

Conclusion

Just as the sun was setting on the evening of Buster's passing, I walked back out onto the front balcony, where our day had begun. As I did, the sky filled with an enormous cloud that looked a little like a dragon, but which I saw as Buster. Calling to Roberto to come and see him it reminded me of how the Ancient Egyptians depicted figures, with two big ears on top of the head side-by-side and a huge mouth open wide. As we watched the movement of the clouds, it appeared as if the one that looked like Buster was expelling something from his mouth, representing the release of the poison that had been inside his body, ultimately causing his demise. As the clouds metamorphosed from pink to grey, we felt a measure of wonder in the midst of our sadness, as if Buster had come to say goodbye and that, for the third and final time that day, the heavens had looked upon us with compassion and grace to let us know that all was well.

Conclusion

As the calendar closed on 2017 after what had been a challenging and emotionally charged year, it was a blessing that I could leave all of that behind. I am also mindful that, just as each day heralds a new beginning, life itself is an ongoing opportunity for release and regeneration. Many, many things have shifted in me as a result of all that I experienced. Unless we take the time to reflect, we miss so much of what is actually unfolding in our lives. Then, there are also times when it is only after the fact that what has transpired and who we have become, can reveal itself to us.

We are never really without anything that we most need and I know we can heal and recover from our wounds and scars, particularly when we are willing to see them as part of the bigger picture and ourselves as one with the thread of humanity. Perhaps the story we've been telling for so long is, in fact, the problem. Now that we are beginning to tell the whole truth of who we are as human beings and how imperfect and vulnerable and fragile we are, we may actually be able to start changing the things that have caused so much pain to humankind throughout time. Let us begin now!

In Peace & Love,
Diane Viola

Buster's Reflections

"That's All Folks!

Life's sweet!

Don't waste a moment!"

Woof, Lick, Kiss!

Buster's Reflections

And as Mummy would say …

"Keep the Puppy Angels with you, look after your body, stay safe, have fun, keep away from the nasty things and I'll see you later alligator.
I Love You Bustie!"

Acknowledgements

Although I have been writing for most of my life, this is the first time I've written an actual book: a profound realisation when it first came upon me! It is indeed a journey in itself and one which, once begun in earnest, I have been eager to complete. Written in 'The Year of the Dog', I felt it was crucial that it be published and launched in 2018 too. I am grateful to everyone who have helped to make that possible.

Topping the list is my husband, Roberto, for whom I have the deepest respect and admiration as a father and for the job he did, as a protector and provider; most importantly of love, to our boy, Buster. His love and support to me has been unconditional. Funny that! There were many times when, overcome with emotion, I would be sobbing as I wrote and he would come running from the other end of the house to comfort me, clearly aware of and empathic toward my pain. (As I write this, I recall that Buster would do exactly the same thing, whereupon I would remind him that Mummy was okay and not to worry.) I am sure everyone who lives with an author would

Acknowledgements

agree, this is, at times, an all-consuming vocation and one where we may well be MIA in the zone. I am grateful for his understanding of my need to devote the time and energy this took and for the limits that placed on our time together when we were both grieving our loss.

My sincere thanks to my friends Jacqueline Booth, Sharron Brandon, Mary Brock, Robert Brown, Vivien Krepp, Beth Phelan, Owen Rigby, Pete Sheldon and Julie Webb, who shared the journey with me and honoured me by reading the manuscript and giving their honest feedback. Their objective appraisal, time and support have been invaluable gifts and each has left their footprint on what you now hold in your hands.

Thanks to Emily Gowor for her enthusiasm for my original concept, and to all the Indie Authors from whom I have learned so much who have helped me to step into this whole new, somewhat scary, world.

To my clients, especially those who knew Buster, I am grateful for your interest and for somehow sensing when I needed time to write. I am also grateful to have had the opportunity to share my stories with you long before they found their way onto the pages of this book and for your positive response to them. To everyone who features in the book as part of the story itself, thank you.

To the RSPCA who gifted us with Buster and who do such amazing work rescuing and re-homing dogs and other domestic animals, and all who cared and provided for Buster over the course of his life, my deepest gratitude.

To my sister-in-law, Elena Viola, my thanks for capturing Buster so beautifully on camera and for the use of her photos on the back cover and the two within this book. And to the young woman who stopped to take what would later become the cover photo, thank you for your kindness and for recording such a precious moment in time.

Acknowledgements

And finally, as much as it breaks my heart that they will not be here to see it, I am truly grateful to my mother, (whose presence I felt throughout the writing) and to my beautiful Buster, who in the same way, gave me the strength and motivation to get this done so that his spirit and teachings could come alive on the page for you to enjoy.

If you'd like to share your thoughts about 'Travels with Buster' to help others find it, your Review on my site www.dianeviola.com/books or your favourite on-line bookstore or Social Media platform would be much appreciated.

Thank You!

About the Author

Diane Viola's passion for humankind and the possibilities inherent in our personal and collective transformation has been at the heart of her work since her own first experience of 'awakening' in 1983. Fortunate to have worked in the Personal Growth field from 1993, and cognisant of the importance of leading by example, Diane has sought to harness her gifts of intuition, compassionate communication, and facilitation to answer the question "How may I serve for the betterment of humanity?".

Opening her private practice as a Relationship & Family Counsellor & Coach in Sydney's Northern Beaches in 1997-1998, she continues to facilitate positive relationships for her global clients from her home on the Gold Coast, Australia.

Along with her earlier work as a teacher, Program Manager for The Peer Support Foundation NSW

About the Author

and Consultant Writer to the Department of School Education NSW, and in her practice as a Master Family & Business Constellations and Emotional Mind Integration Facilitator, Diane has touched the lives of thousands of children, young people, and adults from all walks of life.

An avid writer since her youth, she now takes delight in utilising the power of story and metaphor to touch the heart and soul of the reader, with a second book already in the developmental stages.

To find out more about Diane, her writing and services, or for Workshops or Public Speaker Events, please see

www.dianeviola.com

www.positiverelating.com

or join her

www.facebook.com/DianeViolaAuthor

Notes

www.ingramcontent.com/pod-product-compliance
Lightning Source LLC
Chambersburg PA
CBHW062109290426

4411OCB00023B/2761